TRANSITION

TRANSITION

The Story of How I Became a Man

CHAZ BONO

with Billie Fitzpatrick

DUTTON

DUTTON
Published by Penguin Group (USA) Inc.
375 Hudson Street, New York, New York 10014, U.S.A.
Penguin Group (Canada), 90 Eglinton Avenue East, Suite 700, Toronto, Ontario M4P 2Y3,
Canada (a division of Pearson Penguin Canada Inc.); Penguin Books Ltd, 80 Strand, London
WC2R 0RL, England; Penguin Ireland, 25 St Stephen's Green, Dublin 2, Ireland (a division of
Penguin Books Ltd); Penguin Group (Australia), 250 Camberwell Road, Camberwell, Victoria
3124, Australia (a division of Pearson Australia Group Pty Ltd); Penguin Books India Pvt Ltd,
11 Community Centre, Panchsheel Park, New Delhi–110 017, India; Penguin Group (NZ),
67 Apollo Drive, Rosedale, North Shore 0632, New Zealand (a division of Pearson New Zealand
Ltd); Penguin Books (South Africa) (Pty) Ltd, 24 Sturdee Avenue, Rosebank, Johannesburg 2196,
South Africa

Penguin Books Ltd, Registered Offices: 80 Strand, London WC2R 0RL, England

Published by Dutton, a member of Penguin Group (USA) Inc.

First printing, May 2011
1 3 5 7 9 10 8 6 4 2

𝕫 REGISTERED TRADEMARK—MARCA REGISTRADA

LIBRARY OF CONGRESS CATALOGING-IN-PUBLICATION DATA
Bono, Chaz.
Transition : the story of how I became a man / by Chaz Bono, with Billie Fitzpatrick.
p.   cm.
ISBN 978-0-525-95214-5 (hbk.)
1. Bono, Chaz.   2. Transsexuals—United States—Biography.   3. Transgender people—
United States—Biography.   4. Gender identity—United States—Psychological aspects.
I. Fitzpatrick, Billie.   II. Title.
HQ77.8.B66A3   2011
306.76'8—dc22   2011004279

Printed in the United States of America
Set in Adobe Garamond Pro
Designed by Francesca Belanger

Penguin is committed to publishing works of quality and integrity.
In that spirit, we are proud to offer this book to our readers;
however, the story, the experiences, and the words
are the author's alone.

This book is dedicated to all the kids and teens
of Transforming Family

CONTENTS

CONTENTS

TRANSITION

Prologue

The last image you might have of me is from about ten plus years ago when I was working as a gay and lesbian activist. At that time, I was also writing books (first *Family Outing* and next *End of Innocence*). Then I more or less disappeared.

In my first book, *Family Outing*, I described the events that led to a life-changing moment when I discovered that I was attracted to girls instead of boys, and drew the logical conclusion that I was a lesbian. *Family Outing* also included my mom's side of the story, how she'd had intuitive hunches since I was very young that I might not grow up to be just like her and that I might, indeed, be gay. In that way, *Family Outing* was also a coming out guide; I felt compelled to share my story—not to shock people with a tell-all memoir but rather to reach out to other gay people and their families who were trying to overcome the many challenges of coming out, hoping that they might benefit from my struggle and experience.

Just as I was finishing *Family Outing*, my dad died in a freak skiing accident. I pulled myself together for a couple of years, began writing *End of Innocence*, which was my attempt to make sense of my early music career, its precipitous demise, and my passionate relationship with an older woman. Tragically, Joan died of cancer, after less than two years of powerful love and intense involvement.

These personal losses triggered a gradual but extreme downward spiral in my life that ultimately led me to develop an addiction to prescription painkillers—the only way I found at the time to take the edge off the searing pain inside of me. Though it was a slow progression over many years, my addiction to prescription opiates made it impossible to continue working, and, in fact, I barely made it through writing *End of Innocence*.

My books were heartfelt attempts to give something back to the world and offer something of value to people who might have related to my experiences—coming out, struggling to define a career, or caring for or losing a loved one. As with any project I take on or job I do, I gave all I had to those two books, or as much as I had at the time.

But when I disappeared, drugs and grief were not the only reasons.

The truth is that something very deep inside of me was slowly coming to the surface. Through the pain and sorrow of the loss of both Joan and then my dad; through the frustration and disappointment of my failed music career; through the haze of my dependence on prescription drugs, I began to realize a truth about myself that was so frightening that I became completely paralyzed. In turn, I became so disgusted with my inability to stand up for myself that I retreated further into drugs and the smallest circle of friends and family I could manage.

This truth that was slowly emerging had a hazy beginning. Since I was a child, I'd been aware of a part of me that did not fit. At first, I thought this sense of not fitting in was about me being gay. But as time went on, and I tried different ways of "being a lesbian"—from lipstick to stone butch—I had to admit to myself that the "something" nagging at me was a lot more complicated than just my sexual orientation. Even when I was active in the gay community, I never felt completely at ease. There was something else about me that didn't make sense, something that was much more profound and a lot more threatening. And it took me years to put my finger on what about me felt so disturbing.

This realization didn't happen as a sudden epiphany. No—as with most instances of self-understanding, there were a lot of smaller events that seemed to hint at this larger, more encompassing truth. But the direction that these hints seemed to point to was so frightening and disconcerting that, true as I knew it was, I did everything in my power to shut it down, to deny it, to talk myself out of it, and to block it—with drugs, with ill-fated relationships, with isolation, anything that seemed to push that truth from view.

I can remember going to Washington, DC, while my father was still alive, for the reintroduction to Congress of the Employment Non-Discrimination Act. After his congressional session, my dad took me onto the floor of Congress. I remember thinking at that moment how cool it would be to run for office one day. I began to envision my own career in politics and how proud I'd be to serve my country. But then it occurred to me that I'd have to be called a "congresswoman"—and that one word just stopped me short.

I got a little closer to understanding what was going on with me during my first attempt at sobriety. I recall being at an all-lesbian barbecue with some new friends. At the time, I was involved with a woman who was very social (as well as sober) and I was doing my best to expand my own social life, after being so withdrawn. Newly clearheaded, I still found myself two steps removed from the group, observing their interactions, listening to their stories, and not as engaged as I could have been. And it occurred to me that day: I am not like any of these women. I'm not a femme lesbian; I'm not a jock lesbian; I'm not even a stone butch, despite my mannish shoes and clothing. I had tried on all these quintessential lesbian identities, but none of them had ever really fit. *No,* I thought to myself. *I'm something other, something entirely different.*

Over time, it began to dawn on me that though embodied as a female, I was not a woman at all. That despite my breasts, my curves, and my female genitalia, inside, I identified as a man. This meant, of course, that I was transgender, literally a man living in a woman's body. I have always felt more comfortable wearing boys' and men's clothes. Without a doubt, as a child I thought of myself as a boy. But the process of coming to terms with the reality that I am in fact transgender was horrific. It upended my entire life.

Most of us grow up with the expectation that the way we view ourselves and experience ourselves will eventually make sense. As young children and adolescents, we muddle along, helped and sometimes hindered by those who raise and care for us. We reach adulthood with varying degrees of self-understanding, hoping that a road map to a happy life will emerge. This process of figuring out our lives is never without challenges to overcome, wrong turns, successes and failures. But when something as basic as the physical body doesn't match the internal view we have in our minds, then there is a searing division within the self. And when the sex of the brain and the sex of the body clash, then the only treatment is some form of transition to the other gender. Without this treatment, in my opinion, lives are never fully lived. In many cases, they are shortened by suicide or self-destructive lifestyles.

I am now forty-one years old. This realization, this slow-emerging understanding of myself, became the ultimate motivation to write the book you now hold in your hands.

It would take me almost ten more years before I truly understood the significance of my gender dysphoria, a clinical description that gets to the disconnection between how the body presents its sex and how the brain experiences its sex. In essence, when these two are different (the brain feels itself to be a man but the body is a woman's, and vice versa), the confusion and discomfort is so deep, so disturbing, that most of us try anything to either deny our true feelings or otherwise avoid dealing with ourselves.

Like everyone else on this planet, I grew up in a society of rigid gender roles and had the same distance and lack of understanding about what being transgender really means. I, too, thought it was weird to be transgender. So for years, I fought that secret lurking within me with thoughts such as "Trans people aren't 'normal'—how could they be?" Historically we have been a culture that accepts very little gender variance. Look at our discomfort with feminine men and, to a slightly lesser extent, masculine women. We have plenty of derogatory labels for people who don't fit into our society's strict notions of masculine and feminine: sissy, queen, fairy, butch, dyke, and tomboy, to name a few.

The actual clinical term to define being transgender in the *DSM* IV (the diagnostic manual used by physicians and psychologists) is "gender identity disorder," which still carries with it a certain degree of pathology, not to mention negative connotations. This labeling, this constrained understanding of what it means to be transgender, is only one of many reasons why making the decision to transition is a difficult and often painful conclusion for anyone to reach. Transitioning often leads to loss of jobs, friends, spouses, and family members. And even when relationships aren't severed, they are often pushed almost to breaking points. Before I made my decision to start the process, I was terrified about how all of the people I was close to would handle and feel about my transition. I also had to contend with the fact that, unlike most individuals who transition relatively privately, because I was a public figure with famous parents, my transition would have to take place in front of the whole world. This reality added a pressure to my decision to transition that for years completely incapacitated me.

I was blindsided by the full realization that I'm transgender. I felt completely helpless and paralyzed with fear—at an emotional ground zero. Finally summoning the courage to act on the essential truth about myself was a deep, dark, and often ugly struggle. I had to relive moments of shame, embarrassment, and pain. And yet, though the struggle to start my transition was as frightening and challenging as climbing Mount Everest, I have written this book to show and share with the world something even more remarkable: ever since my first dose of testosterone, I have never felt so whole, so complete, so happy in my life. And this triumph is what *Transition* is all about.

PART ONE

Victim of Circumstance

CHAPTER ONE

A Girl Named Fred

Memory is a tricky thing. Trying to trace back and find the first signs of my being transgender has been quite an interesting, sometimes confounding, and often emotionally painful endeavor. On the one hand, I can tell you that I don't have many clear memories of my early childhood. Like most of us, my earliest explicit memories begin around five years old. But unlike most people, I have stock images stored in my brain that appear as if on cue, presenting the world with facts and pictures that are often already familiar from when I was that cute toddler on my parents' TV show. For years, random people have approached me with their memories of me as a young child, hoping I will share in their enthusiasm and offer a precious pearl of nostalgia from the family vault. What they have never quite understood is that these memories are theirs, not mine.

On a wall in my home, I have a picture of me and my parents in which we're all smiling and looking very happy. I think I am about three in this photo and I'm holding a toy bucket and shovel, so maybe we had been at the beach or a playground sandbox earlier that day.

I look at this photo and others, and I shake my head: I can't remember a single thing from this time in my life. In fact, as this book began to unfold, and I was forced to confront the pain from my life before my transition, I came to realize that many of my early memories are under some kind of psychic lock and key, housed deep in the recesses of my mind, with some part of me standing guard against them. This of course begs a slew of questions, most of which I have finally answered for myself. Some of these relate directly to me being transgender; others relate more to why it was so difficult for me to take the actual step to transition; and still others have simply brought me to a closer understanding of myself as a human being who started out life as a baby girl.

So when I look back on those early years and I see myself as so many did—an adorable baby and toddler dressed in super-girlie clothes of puffy pink dresses, white gingham jumpers, red velvet pantsuits, and blond curls piled up on top of my head—there is a huge disconnect. Yes, I'm smiling. I look happy. I seem to be the center of my parents' adoring attention, but I have no memory of this feeling.

I also have no memory of my parents together, as a couple. Linda, the nanny who took care of me during these early years, was the one person who gave me the warmth, safety, and attention I needed. I was very attached to Linda and trusted her without question. I remember her snuggling me, making my little world fun, and understanding what I needed. Most important, Linda gave me stability. She made me feel safe and loved and always taken care of, which was not something that my parents were able to provide. They worked all the time and just weren't around much. My dad was a total workaholic, and both when my parents were together and for a while after, he kept my mom and himself on a constant schedule. They would tape their television show during the week, and then on weekends, he and my mom would travel to play concerts.

I was almost four when they divorced, and intending to do what was best for me, they decided that I should spend equal time with each of them, trading me off on a weekly basis. Every week I'd have to pack up and move from one house to the other. I remember feeling really sad and scared for the first day or so that I was at my dad's, which was in no way a reflection of how I felt about him, but rather of how the constant moving upset me. There were usually a couple of nights of tears and feeling homesick for my mom's house and Linda, who usually dropped me off and picked me up. After a day or two, I began to adjust and feel comfortable, and once I settled in, I always enjoyed the time that I spent with my dad.

I'm sure some of the difficulty I had with the switching between my parents' homes was because I'd be separated from Linda when I was with Dad, and she had become my security blanket during my parents' divorce. As time went on, I became more used to being shuttled back and forth, but from that point on, I've always dreaded moving, with any relocation triggering a vague sense of uneasiness.

Growing up with superstars as your parents isn't easy. As any child of famous parents will tell you, parents come first. Their careers dominate everything and everyone around you. There is a lot of money involved in everything your parents are doing, and people are paid to attend to the celebrities' needs so that the work—the TV show, recording session, concert, or movie—gets done perfectly. In the midst of all of those commitments, kids can become an afterthought, a person to play or spend time with after everything else is done.

In the absence of royalty, Americans have celebrities.

In my case, I felt kind of lost in the shuffle. Linda was there to ground me, and I knew my parents adored me, but in a general way their celebrity eclipsed everything, including me. As a result, I developed an overwhelming drive to avoid having any kind of emotional needs because they would get in the way of my parents' careers and priorities. This isn't an indictment of my parents, or even celebrity itself; rather it's the reality of the *business* of celebrity.

I had a keen desire to fade into the woodwork so that I would not disturb my parents, distract them from their work, or get in their way. But underneath I think I was very sensitive, a kid who assigned thoughts and feelings to inanimate objects, gave my toys names, and projected all manner of complicated emotional lives on my stuffed animals. Clearly, I see now that I was letting my toys take on the feelings I couldn't let myself have, feelings that I was beginning to tamp down in a regular, automatic way.

This sensitivity also seemed to enable me to attune to the adults around me: I always knew when it was a good time to ask for something, when to garner a smile, and when to disappear. This ability to clue in to adults and their moods and needs actually made me quite self-sufficient at a young age; but it also made me adept at displacing my own needs, a skill that for most of my life has been a sticky issue for me. I have to admit that it took me years to realize I even had my own needs.

One of the clearest memories I have from my childhood is this: I felt like a boy. I may have buried those feelings later, but as a child, they were there.

As soon as I was able to dress myself, my self-image was clear: I chose boys' clothes, boys' shoes and sneakers, and was interested in boys' toys, games, and other preferences. When clothes began to matter more to me, my outfit of choice was usually jeans or cutoffs, sneakers, and football shirts or T-shirts.

At this time, around the age of five or six, my mom and I were living in a big rambling house on Carolwood Drive in Beverly Hills. I went to a nearby school, the Center for Early Education, where all of my friends were boys. At school, I was accepted as a boy—by both the boys and the girls in my class. If a game of tag broke out on the playground, I was always on the boys' team. I thought of myself as a boy among his mates. I dressed like them, ran like them, played like them, smelled like them, and ate like them. I didn't really pay attention to the girls; at this point, they just didn't matter to me. I was part of a miniature rat pack of rough-housing boys and I loved every minute of it.

My being a tomboy didn't bother most anyone. Linda, the parents of my friends, and my teachers all seemed to take my boyishness in stride. Linda herself, though a British nanny, was a bit of a tomboy.

I was a cute little tomboy who was perfectly behaved, got along with other kids, and did everything I was told. I never had the impression that anyone thought I was odd, and I felt nothing but completely accepted as a tomboy. In fact, one of my teachers at the Center for Early Education was Elizabeth Glaser (then Elizabeth Meyer), the Pediatric AIDS Foundation activist who was an early victim of the AIDS epidemic. Elizabeth was also the girlfriend, and later wife of, Paul Michael Glaser, who was then starring in the popular TV show, *Starsky & Hutch*. Since Elizabeth had a special fondness for me and my best friend, Ricky, she often took us to the set to watch them film the show.

Ricky, who I met at this school, and I were inseparable. He was polite and well behaved like me. We loved action figures, Atari, and football. We used to pretend we were American soldiers fighting Germans in the backyard. My friendship with Ricky was easy and effortless. I had no sense of difference between us—we were both boys—and he never gave me any clue that I looked or seemed more or less male than he. I felt completely comfortable with Ricky. He lived in an unremarkable but nice house, in a quiet but kid-filled neighborhood. His parents were not in show business, were still married to each other, and took care of Ricky and his siblings themselves instead of leaving the job to nannies. In short, his life looked a lot like I wished my life would be. I longed to be an average kid leading a normal life, a kid whose parents were not celebrities.

I also loved Ricky's grandfather, who was the captain of the skycaps for one of the major airlines at the time. He often took us to the airport, and we'd hang out with the other skycaps, watch the planes come in, and pretend we were training to be pilots. For two little boys, this was nirvana.

I was active, creative, and good-natured as a kid. I loved playing with our Rottweiler, Hunky, and our Lhasa Apso, China Doll (thus beginning a lifelong, deep-seated camaraderie with animals, and to this day, my relationships with my dogs and cats are fundamental to my life and my peace of mind). I loved to swim and spent hours in the pool. The Carolwood house had a movie theater, and I liked to play in the projection room, pretending that I was editing film and changing reels on my favorite classic horror films, *The Wolf Man* and *Frankenstein*. For my sixth birthday we screened the film *Young Frankenstein* in the theater and gave out rubber monster masks as party favors to all my friends. I also used to like to hang out in a studio apartment on our property and made it into my secret place that I called Dracula's Hideout, a quiet space for myself. There were always so many people and so much stuff going on in my house that I often retreated to my hideout just to get some peace.

My father treated me like the boy I felt myself to be. When I was at his house, I wore boys' clothes, played with boys' toys, and went by the nickname Fred. I became Fred because one day when we were in Uncle Don's, my favorite toy store in Palm Springs, I was looking for a mug or a key ring with my name on it, knowing I was never going to find something that said "Chas," my dad saw my frustration and said, "Let's just pick out a name you like. What about Fred?"

So "Fred" it was, and it stuck. Incidentally, I just found out from my aunt that my nanny Linda also used to call me Fred—clearly I was eager to use my boy name!

From that time on, my dad called me Fred when I was at his house. With both of us in on the joke, our bond became tighter. We would play football in the backyard and he would take me to the horse races. We even wore matching black Pierre Cardin suits to the track. When I think back on the time I spent with my dad, I remember watching a lot of sports—mostly football and tennis—roughhousing in the pool, and hanging out in the kitchen while my dad was cooking dinner. He was still single at the time, and not working very much, so when I was at his house, I got a lot of attention. With my dad, I felt comfortable and happy. Later on, he would become more traditional in his parenting styles. He gave me a definite bedtime and wouldn't let me miss school (something my mom would often do).

I imagined us as a father-and-son team, and this arrangement seemed to work for my dad, too: we both enjoyed doing boy activities, and he never seemed at all bothered by my desire to act and dress like a boy. In fact, I believe that it was more fun for him that I was so masculine rather than a girlie girl. (It seems important to add that I can only speculate as to why my dad felt comfortable allowing me to be myself, which is to say a boy, while I was growing up. I had not yet realized that I was transgender before he passed away, so we never discussed this issue.)

This sense of ease and normality was in direct contrast to how I was beginning to feel at home with my mom. As far back as I remember, my mother always seemed to want me to look and act more like a girl. She made it very clear that she didn't like my masculine style or my preference for only male friends. She often reminded me that she, too, had been a tomboy, as if trying to convince me that I didn't have to stop running around the neighborhood or playing sports, but that I should just choose times and ways to be more feminine.

Thus I began an almost lifelong game of give-and-take with my mom. I could wear jeans and T-shirts, as long as I wore girl's clothes when I had to get dressed up. I could play football, but I also had to take tap and ballet lessons. I could invite all the boys I wanted to my birthday party as long as I invited a few girls. Life with my mother was always a series of complicated, if unspoken, negotiations: "Okay, I'll invite three girls to my party if the theme can be the Cowboys versus the Steelers"; or "I'll wear the Mary Janes to Grandma's house, but the dress is out of the question." No matter who won the argument, I always felt like the loser. I felt that I was not the kind of daughter my mother wanted. Once I returned from my father's wearing a Lacoste shirt he had bought me. It was a boy's polo, and my mother flipped out. She probably thought that my dad encouraged my boyishness rather than that he just let me be myself, which is what I believe he did. The boy I felt I was inside just didn't match what she wanted—or had planned—for her daughter. The fights and, later, snide comments about my clothes, hair, and jewelry lasted into my twenties.

One such negotiation with my mom stands out most. At the beginning of second grade, my mother had bought me a jean skirt with Wonder Woman patches on it. She demanded that I wear it to school. Now, I loved superheroes—but my favorite was the Hulk, certainly not Wonder Woman. I think she actually was trying to institute a wear-a-dress-or-skirt-once-a-week-to-school rule at the time, so she made me wear the skirt.

As I walked down the hall of my elementary school, my friend Jake saw me and quickly came up to me. "What are you wearing?" he asked. He was looking at me like I had two heads. "Why are you dressed like a girl today?"

I was beyond mortified.

After school that day, I told my mother, "I will never ever wear a dress again."

I think this memory is so vivid because in this case I stepped out of my quiet mode and actually voiced my opinion. This was extremely rare for me. My mother must have heard me in a way that she hadn't before, because she never asked me to wear a dress or skirt again. Instead, she'd come up with these dressy pant outfits for any special occasion. My no-dress-wearing rule also applied to any appearance I made on my parents' television show.

Mom and I developed a tacit agreement: I didn't wear dresses or skirts, but I was absolutely not allowed to wear boys' shoes. For some reason, my mom had a real thing about boys' shoes— they just put her over the edge.

To me, my mother has always wanted me to be more feminine. From the moment I was born, she dressed me as a baby, toddler, and young child in a girlie way, and had my bedroom in the Carolwood house decorated in reams of pink. The wallpaper was pink with an Asian-inspired pattern, my bedspread with matching pillow shams was pink, and the carpet, shag of course, was pink as well. I hated this room, hated its girliness and all the pink. But most of all, I hated that I was somehow not the girl my mom wanted me to be.

When my brother was a baby and we were moving out of that house, I finally told my mom that I didn't like the color pink. My next room was much more unisex, decorated in natural tones with wallpaper of tropical foliage and a big log bunk bed that I truly loved. Growing up, all of my rooms were designed by interior decorators, so I never got to have posters on my walls, which was so popular in the seventies. I would have loved to have had in my room a poster of Fonzie, my favorite TV character, or *Rocky*, my all-time favorite movie, or Farrah Fawcett in that red one-piece bathing suit. My friends' walls were all covered with these images, and I envied them—another example of me just wanting to be a normal kid, like my friends.

I was born in 1969 to two iconic entertainers, who introduced me to the country on their hit TV show, *The Sonny and Cher Comedy Hour*. My parents' variety show was one of the most popular shows on TV in the early seventies—like them, it was fresh, hip, and resonated with viewers of all ages. I don't remember much about being on television, but that didn't stop the show from being the defining moment of my life.

For better or worse, since my television debut at the age of two, I have always been and will always be thought of as Sonny and Cher's adorable daughter, Chastity. For better or for worse, my parents' decision to put me on their television show has shaped the course of my entire life. But even I can't believe that that cherubic little girl from the television screen would grow up to be a middle-aged man. But as I think about this vision of me as the "adorable little blond girl," I know that the prevailing ideas about my identity to the public were not just about the clothes I was wearing. My parents were hippies after all, and there were plenty of denim overalls for me and my mom. Rather, it was my sweet demeanor that seemed so feminine.

As I look back on the early years of my childhood, review the events I do remember, and revisit the images of me that are held by others, it occurs to me how tricky not only memory is but gender itself can be. Tricky in the sense of being fluid, gray as opposed to black-and-white, and dynamic instead of static. For much of my life, I have been thought of as that cute little girl from TV, which was so in contrast with how I saw myself. It's a disconnect that has been confusing and awkward—to say the least. This contradiction does not fully explain my gender dysphoria (or my mother's difficulty with it), but it does shed some light on why I took so long to act on this essential part of myself.

During the first three years of my life, my mom's younger sister, my aunt Gee, to whom I've been very close throughout my life, swears that I was a very feminine little girl. Gee lived with us at the time, and she claims, "You were such an angel! An angel baby!"

To this day, Gee and I have ongoing debates about whether I used to be more feminine as a young kid or whether she merely perceived me that way. Since I've transitioned, I've questioned Gee on this point, with her arguing that I was "soft and gentle and sweet and easy—not masculine at all."

Why are *sweet* and *gentle* feminine, I wanted to know. Are these qualities restricted to girls?

As soft and gentle as I might have been, Gee also acknowledged that I had a real rough-and-tumble side to me. Gee remembered, "Well you also did stuff with your dad. You played this game 'Jump Baby Jump' and you'd jump off the refrigerator into your dad's arms."

(Apparently my dad also liked to hang me in the closet to scare people. He'd black out my face with burnt cork and tie me up in a shirt and hang it in the closet. Then he'd ask my mom to get his coat, and when she opened the closet door, there I'd be—hanging in the closet. Clearly, my dad had a weird sense of humor—something that I seemed to have inherited.)

Gender is not always clear.

Many people may not understand how, being born female, I can state with total clarity and certainty that as a child I felt like a boy. That's mainly because most people don't know the difference between gender and gender identity. Gender is the sex that one is born as, and for most of us that sex is either female or male. Your gender identity, however, is based on feelings and not biology. I like to say that your gender identity is between your ears, not between your legs. I am here to attest to the fact that you can be born one sex and yet feel with every fiber of your being that you really are the opposite. And as a kid, it was no more complicated to me than this: I felt like a little boy.

For the vast majority of people in the world, their genders match their gender identities, and so they take it for granted that they mentally and emotionally *feel* like the sex to which they were born. For transgender people, whose bodies are one gender and brains another, life is usually very challenging.

For me, my early certainty that I was a boy began to disappear as soon as I became aware that experiencing myself as male was somehow wrong or problematic. My mother said in my first book, *Family Outing*, that because she didn't know what to make of me or what to do with me, she just kind of ignored me at times. Her need to ignore me was a direct response to her discomfort with my gender identity, a discomfort that I would eventually feel about myself.

But I also think that my mom's behavior—and my response to it—says a lot about how and why I ignored myself for so very long. I had tremendous difficulty allowing for my own needs—and expressing them. I was so used to pushing down my feelings, attuning instead to the needs of others, especially those whom

I most cared about, that I was consumed with worries about how everybody else would feel if I transitioned. When I finally did realize I was transgender, I had to overcome forty years of putting others ahead of myself before I had the guts to take my first step, an act that has become a crucial life lesson.

CHAPTER TWO

Puberty: The First Time

I find it kind of ironic that I'm calling this book *Transition*. Though I made what some may view as a huge transition going from female to male, change of any kind has always been difficult for me. I am a creature of habit to the nth degree. If I find an item I like on a favorite menu, I always order that dish. The same can be said about the car I like to drive, the hotels where I like to stay, the theaters where I prefer to see movies, the places where I like to vacation, and most important, where I choose to live. I have lived in my present house for six years and have no plans for moving. I lived in my previous home for eight years. Surely some of my dislike of change comes from having it forced upon me during so much of my childhood and youth. Shuttling between my parents' homes after their divorce was just the beginning. When I was about seven and my mom got married to Gregg Allman when she became pregnant with my brother, she moved us out of the Carolwood house and into one on Linden Drive in Beverly Hills. Soon after, we moved again to Malibu Colony, then back to an apartment on Wilshire Boulevard in Westwood, and then to the Sea Colony in Santa Monica. For anyone who understands the layout of Los Angeles, this is quite a road map.

My mother has always liked to buy properties, redo the

interiors, and then sell and move on. This is the way that my mom grew up. In much the same way, her own mother, who was married seven times, moved my mom and my aunt Gee around often throughout their lives.

My mom's habit of moving seems to be natural for her, one so familiar that she probably didn't stop and think of it as potentially negative for anyone else. But for me, every move was unsettling, even if I didn't realize it at the time. For about six years—from age six to age twelve, I probably moved a half dozen times. In between the more interim homes, we also stayed at the Beverly Hills Hotel. I literally can't remember how many month-long stays we had at the Beverly Hills Hotel. My mom always liked to live in a nice environment; she is very visual and is talented at designing and decorating. In fact she has helped me decorate all of my homes. I think she sees her home as an extension of herself and wants to be in a setting that feels comfortable. So even if the home was temporary, she liked to put her stamp on it, too.

This may all sound kind of glamorous, but it wasn't for me. The novelty of living in a hotel wore off fast. I don't even remember packing or unpacking, so that must've been done for me by people my mother hired. And I didn't look at moving as an adventure *or* a hardship really—it was just an uncomfortable fact of my life. I didn't understand that most people didn't live this way.

In my typical fashion, I just rolled with it all and never complained, despite my internal feelings. In truth I don't even think I acknowledged to myself that it bothered me. Moving just became a part of life and I tried not to get too attached to any place we were living; it was a matter of emotional practicality.

My brother Elijah was born when I was seven, and my mom hired a new baby nurse to care for him. Soon after, my beloved nanny Linda stopped working for us. Linda was my one constant after the upheaval of the divorce, and I completely depended on her for emotional support. With her gone, I lost my sense of security and safety, and I was devastated. Then while my mom, Elijah, and I were away in Japan on tour with the Greg Allman Band, my mom got word that the baby nurse had quit. She called my dad and asked him if he could find a replacement since we were so far away.

When we arrived back in LA, we met the new nanny, Harriet.

On the surface, Harriet seemed quite respectable, a registered nurse, a mature woman, even matronly. Harriet was short with red hair and freckles, though her face was set in a permanent scowl. I'm serious. Though she was probably only in her forties, she seemed ancient compared to everyone around me. She was in charge of both me and Elijah, who, let's just say, was a challenge.

Elijah got into trouble regularly. Unfortunately, in some weird twist of Harriet's psyche, anytime Elijah would really act out, she punished me. Mind you, Elijah was just two or three years old at the time, so his infractions were hardly criminal. Still, I suffered the wrath of Harriet's frustration with my brother. I remember one classic example after spending a weekend at my grandmother's house with my brother, during which my brother had behaved exceptionally badly.

During the middle of the night, Harriet woke me up three separate times to scream at me. Yelling in an angry, vindictive way, she told me that because I was so bad, my grandmother was furious with me and was never going to let me come and stay with her again. Of course this was not true, and I knew even then that Harriet was simply trying to upset me and make me doubt my connection to my grandmother and her boyfriend, Craig, to whom I was especially close. Craig was a major figure throughout most of my early years; he was a real man's man and I just adored him. He was very handsome, tall, and muscular, with a full beard. I used to wish I could have a beard like his when I grew up. We used to play handball for hours behind my grandmother's quilt store; he took me to the movie *Rocky*, and even taught me how to punch a heavy bag.

One of Harriet's favorite forms of torment was to go through my desk drawer, not find it neat enough, then dump the contents of all my drawers and my closet, including all the clothes, in the middle of the floor of my room and tell me to put everything back in its place. She also had all my T-shirts and sweatshirts made with my name on the back (football jersey style) and then told me that I would be kidnapped by someone because they would know who I was. This put me even more on edge then I normally was.

Thirty years later, I now understand that Harriet, probably, was mentally ill. Like most people who suffer from mental illness, she was not *always* abusive, and sometimes seemed almost like a normal nanny. As if to encourage me to let down my guard, she could even be sweet. For my eleventh birthday, she and her husband (after coming to work for us, she married my mother's chauffeur) took me and a couple of my friends on a ski trip to Big Bear Mountain in California. Her husband was the nicest guy in the world, and we had a blast on this trip—skiing and inner-tubing.

But usually the very next day, after having seemed so happy and relaxed, Harriet would act out, humiliating me by making me wear my hair up or in a bun because it was a hot day, or grounding me, not letting me play outside, watch TV, or even go swimming—all for fictitious infractions.

Even scarier, I felt completely isolated and unable to protect myself from Harriet. Like most kids who suffer some kind of abuse, I was afraid to tell anyone what was going on. And of course, I hated to complain. I didn't want to make trouble. The only time I went to my mom and tried to explain what Harriet was doing and how she was treating me, my mother said, "If you're having a problem with Harriet, then you're going to have to work it out with her."

I hadn't explained what exactly Harriet was doing, and I'm sure that my mom thought I was just upset with Harriet for trying to discipline me. Why would my mom think anything else? On the surface, Harriet seemed reasonable and responsible, not at all suspicious. It was also just like my mom not to want to intervene in a conflict that did not directly involve her.

But in my child's brain, the take-away from my mom's response was that I had to suffer through it.

Upon hearing about Harriet's treatment of me, people have asked me why I didn't just go and live with my father, or at least spend more of my time at his house. I think the reasons are threefold. As far back as I can remember, I'd always wanted a baby brother; when Elijah came along, I was thrilled and never wanted to be apart from him, which was the primary reason why I had begun to see less of my dad by this time. I also think that

I felt protective of Elijah, knowing at some level that Harriet was dangerous, especially to my brother, who was so young and even more vulnerable than I. And finally I think that I just didn't question my circumstances; I was being raised to soldier on, in spite of any adversity.

One of the more enjoyable aspects of my life at this time, in spite of Harriet, was when I went on tour with my mother. From when I was nine until I was thirteen, my mother had a nightclub act at Caesar's Palace. So we'd spend part of every summer in Las Vegas and then go on the road. We went to Atlantic City, Monte Carlo, South Africa—all very cool places, and I loved it.

Being on tour with my mom and her show meant that I got to hang out with the singers and dancers, who were like a second family to me, and one that made me feel very much at ease with myself and completely accepted. As a kid, I generally got along better with adults than with my peers, and while on tour with my mom, I felt a special kinship to the gay dancers and female impersonators who toured with her. I can remember when I was about nine, I asked my mom's assistant, Deb, why these men dressed up like women; she explained that this was their profession, and that dressing up was the way that they per-formed. Once I met these guys and saw them on stage, I never gave what they did another thought—I just loved it—and have been a fan of female impersonators ever since. I can't say that I was making a conscious connection between these gay drag queens and my gender confusion; I was just naturally drawn to the gay dancers and female impersonators. And they let me hang out and tag along when they'd go shopping or out to lunch. Unfortunately not everybody was as open-minded about the dancers. Harriet was incredibly homophobic and often reminded me that the dancers were "queer" and told me that when they were up on stage, they were not really concentrating on their performance, but rather scanning the audience for who they are going to f___ that night. She actually used this word with me, a then-ten-year-old. Harriet even tried to convince my mother to send me away to boarding school.

Life on the road was a blast, but I dreaded those Sunday nights during the school year when I had to go home to Harriet. I would always try to talk my mom into letting me stay in Vegas and miss school on Monday, which she would often do. It was truly hard to leave my mom and everybody on tour to have to go back home with Harriet. I always felt more afraid of her when my mom wasn't around. And even though my mom gave me flack about my masculine demeanor and criticized how I dressed, I felt better when she was at home because I knew that if anything ever went horribly wrong with Harriet, my mom would be there to stop it.

From about age seven to ten, when I was attending the Center for Early Education, I was still friends with Ricky, and still generally at ease in my body and identifying as a boy. But by the end of third grade, I had missed so much school from going on tour with my parents, and then later with mom, that I was really behind for my grade. My mom was told that I would probably do better at a school that could help me catch up; unfortunately, this new school specialized in educating children with both learning differences and behavioral and emotional issues.

The classes at this new school were really small, with eight to ten kids per class. One kid in particular stands out because of the temper tantrums he threw; he had to be carried out of the class—it was very disturbing for everyone else. I remember clearly that when the behaviorally disturbed kids had outbursts or acted out, they were taken out and put into the quiet room (in isolation) until they calmed down. We were all terrified because we didn't really understand how these kids were different. There were kids on Ritalin (one kid told me he took speed), but this was in the really early days of diagnosing ADD. I also didn't have *any* friends at school. I mean that. None.

Needless to say, this environment made me very uneasy, and at some point during this time, I was sent to a child psychologist to help with my nervousness. Even given the struggles I was having, I never voiced my discomfort about anything. I never told anyone that the place felt like an insane asylum to me. I never explained that being in this environment was giving me so much anxiety I couldn't keep my lunch down most days.

Even back then I knew it was completely illogical, if not damaging, for the school to specialize in both learning difficulties and behavior problems, two very separate types of problems. Being around kids who had severe behavioral issues really stressed me out—so much that I developed a nervous stomach condition that would often make me sick at school. And even sadder, I didn't need to be there. I didn't have any kind of learning difference; I was simply behind for my grade as a result of being taken out of school so often. Even so, the damage was done: school became a place where I felt stupid, where I felt I didn't fit in, and where I felt a gnawing dread and anxiety that permeated my mind and body.

As I got older, Ricky and I started to slowly and naturally grow apart. We were less interested in playing our boyish games, and I was feeling a need to talk and express myself verbally in a way that Ricky didn't seem as interested in. Right before I turned nine, I met a new friend, Gina. She was three years older than me and the younger sister of our weekend babysitter, Colleen, who was a college student at Pepperdine, near our house in Malibu. Colleen came to our house on Harriet's days off, and once she suggested to my mom that she bring along her little sister, who she thought would get along with me.

Gina and I hit it off at once. On the very first day she came to play, we were down on the beach running around and she broke her toe on a log. We had to take her to the ER, and the two of us were worried that her mom would never let her come over again. Everything was fine, of course, and after that, Gina and I were practically inseparable, and most weekends we spent together alternating between houses. We soon had nicknames for each other that we still use to this day. Gina became Beans, because she was tall and skinny like a string bean, and I was Bones, a play on my last name.

Gina lived in Newbury Park, a typical middle-class neighborhood about an hour's drive from Malibu. The main difference between Ricky and Gina was that I could really talk to Gina, in a way that I never did with Ricky. I think this says something about female versus male development in adolescence—girls are much more verbal during this time. In this way, I guess I was becoming a bit more feminine. My relationship with Ricky was more physical—it was about playing and doing. As talking became more vital to me, I found myself gravitating more toward Gina.

Though Gina was a girl, she was not at all frilly or feminine; she was a typical tomboy—a great athlete, into skateboarding and riding bikes, and not preoccupied with boys. In these ways we had a lot in common. I loved to spend time at her house; similar to how I felt hanging out with Ricky, I loved staying at Gina's, where I could feel normal, just riding skateboards and hanging out with the other kids on her street. Perhaps my desire for normalcy was just my way of rebelling against my parents; but perhaps, too, I knew, even as a child, that Hollywood and show business weren't real. I was kind of a seeker even back then, and what I sought after most was reality. Even today, though I'm not quite as dogmatic about it, I still see myself as a normal everyday guy who has lived some unusual moments.

Then, my body started to change.

The first time I started to hit puberty—or puberty hit me—I was horrified.

I was young when puberty started—only about eleven, and this made me miserable. Of course, my mother and Aunt Gee had told me about puberty—but nothing could quite prepare me for my body's changes. Most young people can't wait to develop and evolve into adults. I hadn't dreaded puberty; in fact I hadn't thought about it at all. I just ignored my body until the inevitable occurred. I could no longer just wear T-shirts and gym shorts after school. I could no longer pretend that I looked just like a boy; I was turning into a woman.

One day in sixth grade, right as I was about to turn twelve,

Harriet informed me that I needed to start wearing a bra. Clearly, I needed to be told; I certainly didn't ask for one. I don't remember the exact conversation, but I do remember Harriet taking me to a department store where she picked out a couple of bras. Right after, I went to Gina's house for the weekend. It was my first time wearing the bra, and I remember constantly tugging on it, trying to arrange it in a way that wouldn't feel so uncomfortable. Honestly, it wasn't just that this was something I needed to get used to; I hated having to wear it at all, because it felt so unnatural to me. Wearing a bra felt like a smack in the face—a blatant reminder that I was not the boy I felt I was. I wanted a boy's reedy lines, sharply defined muscles, strength and power— all the things I associated with being a boy. Instead my body was giving me soft curves and a shape that I hated more and more with each day. And my breasts seemed to grow even faster. At twelve I was wearing a C bra cup, and by the time I was fully mature at eighteen I was wearing a double-D. I always felt my breasts were enormous, foreign appendages, and I spent considerable energy throughout my adolescence, as well as most of my adult life, trying to hide my breasts behind baggy high-cut shirts and minimizing bras.

When I got my period later the next year, I was at the movies with my aunt. We'd gone to see *Fame*, and during a restroom break, I noticed that I was bleeding. Instead of the red tide that I'd expected, I saw only dark brown spotting. I was horrified. The blood was a sign of doom, of weakness, of something I didn't want at all. Later that same year, when I used my first tampon, Harriet told me that I would only need one slender size for the whole school day. I was in seventh grade, and I ended up bleeding all over my uniform skirt and all the kids made fun of me, even after I changed into my gym shorts.

Most of the other girls seemed really excited about going through puberty. Not me—I was horrified by what was happening to me and couldn't relate to the other girls at all. For those of us who are gender dysphoric, puberty is a time of tremendous pain and discomfort. I've found this to be true not only in the research I've done but also in the one-on-one conversations I've had with many female-to-males, which is why, as I've begun working with trans youth, I've seen that it's more and more common for them to wish to go on hormone blockers before puberty starts.

As with many FTM adolescents, my periods were painful to the point of being debilitating. In my later teens, my periods became so extreme that I had to be heavily medicated and couldn't get out of bed for the first day or so of my cycle. My female reproductive organs gave me many years of pain and complications—both physical and emotional. Doctors found precancerous cell growth on my cervix, multiple endometrial cysts on my ovaries (at one time reaching the size of a golf ball), and then another cyst in my uterus in my later twenties. After numerous surgeries, and an almost lifelong battle with gynecological pain, I finally had my uterus removed when I was thirty-six.

I believe the fact that I had so many problems with my female reproductive organs was my body's way of demonstrating how those parts had never really belonged in my body in the first place. My female reproductive parts caused me as much physical pain as being trapped in a female shell caused me emotional and spiritual pain.

Right before sixth grade, we moved again; this time to Santa Monica. The good news was that I left school and got to go to a great Montessori school, where I felt right at home. I loved the open, creative atmosphere and made many friends, even becoming class president. Life was good. My mom still got on my case about being too masculine and not wearing the "right" clothes, but I was learning how to navigate her criticisms. I stuck to guy shorts and jeans, which seemed to pass muster. In general, I was just relieved to be out of that previous school.

At the end of the sixth grade, the house in Benedict Canyon that my mom had been building from the ground up was finally ready and we moved again. I also had to change schools again because the Montessori school only went up through sixth grade. This time, I was going to Curtis, an upright prep school, which required girls to wear a strict uniform of a skirt, jacket, and blouse. The moment I arrived on campus, I knew in my gut that this was not going to be a good place for me. It wasn't just the constricting uniform that didn't fit, the general tenor of the school was completely opposite of my personality. I was a black-leather-jacket-Nike-sneaker-wearing tomboy, and the girls at Curtis appeared to me to be stuck up and only interested in boys and shopping. My differences led me to be teased daily by the boys in my class. They had taken to calling me Balboa, after my hero Rocky, because of a bump on my nose, which I got as a child when it was broken during a Little League game. I had gone from being one of the guys, to being rejected and ridiculed by them on a daily basis.

To make matters more stressful, Curtis was also more

academically rigorous than anything I'd ever experienced. I immediately began struggling to keep up with the workload, and I had to have a tutor work with me several times a week. Even with extra help, I could barely keep my head above water. Curtis was about one thing and one thing only—academics. There was nothing else to interest me or to build up my confidence. There were no arts programs of any kind, no theater or music classes. And there was barely an athletic program. During the seventh grade the only person that I made friends with was the girls' gym teacher, who was most likely a lesbian.

Then in the middle of seventh grade, fortune finally smiled on me. My mother had been trying to become an actress for several years, but no one in the business had been taking her seriously. Unlike today, in the early eighties, singers like my mom didn't become serious film and theater actors. After years of her trying to act, director Robert Altman finally took a chance and offered my mom a role in his Broadway play (which would later be made into a film), *Come Back to the Five and Dime, Jimmy Dean, Jimmy Dean*, and we got the chance to move to New York for six months.

This was a huge break for my mom, and ended up becoming a big break for me as well. I immediately fell in love with New York, and more important, Harriet didn't come with us.

In the city, my mother enrolled me at the Walden School on the Upper West Side, full of the children of liberal New York City parents, and I felt right at home there. I loved living in the city, going to Central Park, riding the subway to movies downtown. New York City kids have a tremendous amount of freedom because of public transportation. The city felt like an enormous playground to me, where I felt free and unencumbered. I could go wherever I wanted without having to wait for a grown-up to drop me off or pick me up. I could hop on a bus or a train and go meet some school friends at a museum, a coffee shop, or the park. I had no nanny that I felt was persecuting me, and my mom was busy with work. All of this independence made me feel grown-up. I felt alive and energetic in a way that I had never experienced before. I felt like I had been reborn.

It was in New York that I finally got the courage to tell my mom about what Harriet had been doing to me for the past five years. We were staying in a top-floor apartment at the Mayflower Hotel. We were hanging out, sitting in my mom's room on her bed, and I told my mom very matter-of-factly that if Harriet came back when we went home to Los Angeles, I was going to live with my dad. I didn't go into any more detail. I thought, perhaps, that my mom didn't really want to hear the long, sordid drama. But I must have made my point, because I never saw Harriet again.

A couple of years later, I did finally share with my mom all of what Harriet had done and how she had treated me. I think what had finally enabled me to speak up about Harriet's abuse was an incident that happened right after my mom had left for New York but before my brother and I had joined her. Harriet had gotten it in her head that because my English teacher let me make up a test that I had missed when I was home sick, I was getting special treatment. Harriet had become so irrational that she called the school principal and told him that the English teacher should be fired. I had tried to explain to her that my classmates had already taken the test, and that I was given only one more day than they were to study and then make up the test.

But Harriet wouldn't listen and did everything she could to try to get my teacher fired. I talked to my teacher to apologize. The whole thing was crazy, and it was the first time I really understood, from an older perspective, that there was something seriously off about Harriet. I had been terrified until I finally got to New York.

Of course, my mom was shocked when she heard about Harriet and had had no idea she was abusive. Several years later a woman came up to my mom while we were on vacation in Aspen. She was from the same town as Harriet and had known her there. She wanted to let my mom know that she thought Harriet had lied to us about her past and the circumstances that had led her to leave the Midwest and come to work for us. We thought that Harriet had a son who had recently died of leukemia and that's why she had moved to LA. According to this women, Harriet had a daughter and son who were the same age as my brother and me, and not only were they both alive, but Harriet had had some kind of nervous breakdown and abandoned her husband and children. Most important, this woman wanted to make sure Harriet was no longer working for my family or in charge of children.

Transitions have always been hard for me. The back-and-forth between my parents' homes when I was younger; the constant moves from house to house with my mom; even the extremely enjoyable times that I spent on tour with her, which always ended with me going back to LA, and the short time I lived in New York, where I felt so free and at peace, finally away from my nemesis Harriet—all of this reinforced a sense of not being rooted. As a child, this sense of rootlessness was a reflection of the logistics of my particular childhood. But as I got older, as my body took on the shape of a woman in ways I wasn't comfortable with, the rootlessness felt more like it was inside of me.

In some ways the constant moving may have helped me stay away from the growing discomfort inside of me, the deep knowing that there was something not quite right about me. Harriet's treatment of me definitely exacerbated my discomfort with myself; as any victim of abuse (emotional, physical, or sexual) will attest, we take on the abuse as if there is something wrong with us.

But my own vulnerability, my own private disconnect between my mind and my body was developing, just as I was.

One instance that really spells this out comes to mind. In the late seventies, when my brother was about a year old and I was eight or nine, my parents got together to do a few weeks of shows at the Rye Hilton in New York. I went with them, as did a young twentysomething student teacher who worked at my school and was to be tutoring me.

I don't remember the young woman's name, who was also with us on the trip. The tutor and I often hung out in my hotel room, supposedly doing schoolwork. One day she started playing a game with me: I was her boyfriend and she was my girlfriend. I remember being in bed together with our shirts off, dry humping, kissing, and cuddling.

I was with her in bed before her date, and I remember feeling jealous of him and telling her that I wanted to be her only boyfriend. I also remember her telling me not to tell my parents about what was going on. I instinctively knew what we were doing was bad or wrong. But next to this knowledge of the illicitness was pleasure, which led me to feel very confused and guilty for a long time.

This incident left me feeling like the perpetrator, something I no longer believe or feel. But though clearly this was sexual abuse, the event wasn't terribly traumatic for me. It never happened again. What strikes me most now about it is how natural it was for me to play the male role.

CHAPTER THREE

Am I a Lesbian?

In March, I celebrated my thirteenth birthday in New York, and my mom surprised me and flew in Gina. We went to go see the movie *Personal Best*, starring Mariel Hemingway, which had just opened. When the two women began to kiss up on the big screen, I came to a startling realization about myself: I was a lesbian.

Watching the women embrace made a light go off in my head and I thought, *That is what I want to do*. I wanted to kiss and touch a girl just like the women in the movie were doing. The only logical cause for this feeling was that I had to be a lesbian.

Immediately, I felt a haze recede: I had finally found the reason I felt so different from most girls my age—or at least I thought so at the time. I also felt that I now understood why I was such a tomboy, why I didn't like girlie toys as a kid, why I liked to dress the way I did, and why I had preferred boys as friends. Being a lesbian seemed to explain so much: why I wanted to wear men's clothing, preferred men's shoes, and didn't like my female body, especially my breasts.

I see now that I was looking outside myself to understand who I was—like any teenager, I was looking and hoping to recognize myself in someone else. I was now so happy and relieved to think that I had finally answered the looming question of who I was. I thought identifying as a lesbian answered every aching question I had about myself.

At the time, and for many years after this point, this conclusion made the utmost sense. Now I realize that I was wrong—yet another example of the trickiness of not just memory but perception, especially about the self.

Of course, I now see that what I was relating to most was the sexuality on screen: I had skipped over the gender piece of the puzzle. This conclusion and confusion is quite common among FTMs. The majority of the trans-men that I know have, at some point in their lives, identified as lesbians and spent time in that community. But the key is that we also imagine ourselves to be boys in our fantasies. When I was first experimenting sexually, I was always in the male role. I would play house with girls and pretend that I was the husband and my friend was the wife. Interestingly, my role as the man in these situations was never in question or disputed by the girl with whom I was playing. It's so easy for young children to be exactly who they want to be and be accepted by their peers, before we are forced to realize that society has certain rules when it comes to these situations.

Throughout high school and into my early twenties, identifying as a lesbian helped define me. At last I had some answers, felt a sense of belonging to a community, and I finally began to feel comfortable in myself.

It took me thirty years to disentangle my sexual orientation and my gender identity. I was born in a female body and I was sexually attracted to women; therefore the only explanation for this was that I was a lesbian. The idea that I was really male, despite the fact that I inhabited a female body, was so foreign to me that even though that truth had been staring me in the face ever since I could remember, I denied it for the vast majority of my life.

After spending a blissful six months in New York, I finished up the school year and we moved back to LA. My mom had one more summer to play in Vegas and we moved back into the Benedict Canyon house, an all-white Egyptian-style house, with a Plexiglas portion of roof that slid out over an indoor courtyard. The front door also slid open, like an elevator door, when you pushed a button. My mom lived in that house until I was in my early twenties, when she decided to move back to Malibu. I honestly miss that house and wish my mother still lived there, though I understand her desire to live by the ocean.

With Harriet gone, living at home was more comfortable. But walking the halls of the Curtis School was still a lonely affair. In fact, since the school was under renovation, the campus was a muddy mess, and most of my classes were set up in temporary trailers. This only added to my discomfort. The problem wasn't that we were studying in trailers, but that we no longer had a formal gym class (which had always been my favorite class) and the school had shrunk in size. The school seemed even more homogenous and claustrophobic. I was now in eighth grade, and the campus was made up of only seventh and eighth graders, making it more difficult to disappear. There were fewer kids, fewer teachers, and fewer opportunities for me to find friends. Girls' gym was now taught by the English teacher and entailed running around outside in the mud or doing stretches. My one friend, the girls' gym teacher, had gone. I felt totally lonely and isolated.

I was also now completely absorbed in being gay and trying to fit into whatever that meant. That summer, I had come out to Gina, which was pretty effortless. Gina was completely unfazed by my sexual orientation, and that was a huge weight off my chest to finally tell somebody. I was also relieved that my coming out to Gina didn't seem to change our relationship in the least. What we had in common had nothing to do with sexual orientation.

But as supportive as Gina was, she wasn't gay. I didn't know anyone else my age who was gay. Sure, I now knew that some of the men in my mother's show were gay—and figured that this was why I liked hanging out with them so much. Otherwise I felt a little stranded. And keep in mind: this was in the early eighties—no gay TV characters, and very little gay information, outreach, or support was available. On this subject, the world was a virtual information wasteland. I thought that the only place to meet other gay people was in a gay bar, and I therefore made the assumption that I wouldn't find a girlfriend or meet any gay kids until I was twenty-one. I remember being really envious that all the other kids my age could go steady or make out. In fact, I thought I wouldn't even have my first kiss for eight more years, when I'd finally be able to get into a gay bar.

My only refuge was the screenplay I was pouring every feeling and free minute into writing. It was about a lesbian basketball player who falls in love with one of her teammates. I titled it *Jump Shot*; the plot was essentially the same as *Personal Best*, but used basketball instead of track as a backdrop. This was 1982, and I had no access to information about gay adolescence, so I relied on my imagination and my own burgeoning sexuality to fill out the scenes and create a story. I never got very far, but I worked on it constantly, on a typewriter in the dark of my room, always keeping the typewritten pages at hand. Of course my family was curious and kept asking to read my grand opus, but I wouldn't show them. I'd written a theme song to *Jump Shot* as well, but that, too, was for my ears only. The only person I shared it with was Gina. She was a great athlete and an even better sport about indulging me.

Since transitioning, I've been back in touch with Gina and we laughed about *Jump Shot*, and how obsessed I was with writing it. Apparently, I would make her sit with me while I was in front of a typewriter, working, intermittently asking her to read the script. Gina also reminded me that even when we were teenagers, I told her that I didn't feel comfortable in my body.

Then I fell in love.

It was Christmas of 1982 and I was thirteen. That year, my mom had a tree-decorating party at her house. A bunch of us were up in my mom's bedroom watching a tape of an HBO special that she had just done. I was sitting on the floor when in walked a woman whom I recognized but couldn't immediately place. She was tall, blond, and gorgeous. It was Joan, an old friend of my mother's, whom I had first met in Las Vegas when she came up to visit my mom while she was performing there. I had always known Joan was a lesbian, but now I saw her through new eyes, and I felt as if she could see right through me.

Joan and my mom had met briefly when they were seventeen,

45

through their mutual friend, Della, and had gotten to know each other better a few years later when Joan started dating an older woman named Scotti, who was also friends with my grandmother's best friend. My mom had lost contact with Joan and Scotti for over a decade but had reconnected when I was about nine. Then Joan and Scotti became a regular part of our extended family of friends, accompanying us on summer vacations to our house in Aspen. And after that they were always invited to parties or barbecues at our house. Sometimes just my mom and Joan would hang out, go shopping, or spend a girls-day-out together.

That night I didn't let Joan out of my sight. She was dressed in a sexy black leather skirt and red silk blouse, and I thought she looked stunning. I was used to hanging around with adults, and I tried everything in my thirteen-year-old head to entertain her. Joan had a date (she and Scotti had broken up many years earlier, but continued to live together, like family), but that didn't stop me from following her around the entire evening. I talked to her, told her jokes, anything to get and keep her attention.

After the Christmas party, I sought out Joan and began to call her on my own just to chat or suggest we go out for lunch. And even though I had a huge crush on her, I mostly looked up to her as an older adviser who happened to be a lesbian. She became the first adult lesbian in my life who gave me a strong sense of hope that all was going to be okay. Joan was loving, consistent, and loyal and was somebody I could always turn to and talk about whatever was on my mind—otherwise confidants were few and far between for me. As an older teen I'd spend time with Joan and her friends any chance I got. Joan only dated super-butch women, and all of her lesbian friends seemed to fall into butch-femme pairs, as did Joan herself, who was hyper-feminine and sexy. Joan's girlfriend at that time was a woman named Dori, whose best friend was Suzanne. Both Dori and Suzanne were very masculine stone-butch type dykes, and I totally related to them. Joan used to say that Dori was her James Dean, and I could see what she meant—Dori was cool. She was tall, thin, and always dressed in a traditionally masculine way. She was also kind of standoffish, radiating a masculine self-confidant vibe.

Suzanne, or Suzs, was much more kid friendly and we became fast friends. When I met my first girlfriend Shara, at fourteen, it was Suzs who took me aside and told me how to make love to a woman.

I was very attuned to the kind of relationships that Joan and her friends seemed to have, those classic old-school butch-femme relationships, which made sense to me from the start. I remember looking up to the women that she dated and thinking, "That's how I want to be when I grow up." I wanted to express my identity in the same masculine way. And Joan, unlike anybody else I knew, seemed to be attracted and connected to the women that she dated because of those masculine attributes. It was inevitable that Joan would soon become the object of my affection—not only was she a beautiful feminine woman, but she was the only adult woman I knew who thought there was nothing wrong with masculine women. In short, being around Joan and her friends gave me hope for my future. Joan's femininity and her very masculine girlfriends were the closest I came (perhaps unconsciously) to gender roles that made sense.

Through my teenage years and into my early twenties Joan

came to be as important to me as Linda had been when I was a child. Joan opened her house to me and her loving heart, both of which gave me a sense of stability and consistency that I desperately needed.

For my fourteenth birthday, my mom gave me another exceptional gift: she sent me to the Lee Strasberg Theatre & Film Institute in West Hollywood, first for the youth weekend program and then for the summer program. When she first told me that she had enrolled me at Strasberg, I didn't want to go. I had no interest in acting and I didn't want to spend my weekends taking acting classes. But my mom insisted, and I was glad she did.

I think she saw that I was very unhappy in school and that I didn't have any friends. I think she probably thought that I would enjoy doing something more creative and that a drama class might offer me more opportunities to meet kids I actually related to. And she was right.

I took to the school immediately, and I made friends fast. I loved everything about acting—the role-playing, the complete absorption in a scene or script, the creative freedom to leave my body, my personality, and my self. Similar to how I felt hanging with the cast in my mom's Vegas show, I found myself relaxed and happy in a way that had completely eluded me at Curtis. I took acting, dance, and singing lessons and performed in two shows. At the wrap party for one of the shows, I kissed my first girl, or to be more accurate, she kissed me. At the house party, I was standing in the kitchen talking to my friend Shara, who was a model. Suddenly, Shara pinned me against the refrigerator and kissed me. I was so overwhelmed and made so nervous by her actions that I didn't know how to respond. But it didn't take me long to figure it out. Fairly soon after, Shara and I were sneaking off to make out as much as we could.

It was a truly fantastic summer. I was living with my mom, going to Strasberg during the day, and working at Bono, my dad's newly opened Italian restaurant, three nights a week, bussing dirty dishes. I was also reconnecting with my dad, and making more cash than I'd ever had before. I loved knowing that I'd earned it versus having it given to me; it made me feel great. Plus, there was the access to the great food. My dad and I became very close again, and the nature of our relationship changed into a more mature understanding of each other. My father began to feel less like a parent and more like an ally to me.

This experience actually turned my life around. I ended up having this very rich summer, meeting more kids (up till then, my only friend was still Gina). Before this my summers had always been about going on tour with my mom. Now, as I was going into becoming a teenager, it was all about me and hanging with kids who were creative and of my own age.

It was also during that summer, probably as a result of loving the movie *Fame,* that I came up with the idea of going to the High School of Performing Arts (or PA as everyone called it) in New York City, a public alternative high school for teens gifted in music, dance, or drama. My time at Strasberg had given me confidence and made me believe that I might actually be good at acting. I was also desperate to get back to NYC, and I thought if I went to school there I would find the same kind of camaraderie

I had at Strasberg. I believed that all the difficulties I'd had with school would disappear in a place that was so open, creative, and accepting. Soon I became single-minded about getting into PA and began to bug my mother relentlessly about applying. Finally I convinced her to check out the school on a trip to New York. She came back impressed, but wary—she didn't want me to get my hopes up because she'd found out that thousands of kids auditioned every year, but only two hundred were accepted. Getting accepted into PA was no sure thing. But I was determined.

At the end of the summer, I flew to New York with our family friend, Randy Rocca, to audition. I had to have two contemporary monologues prepared for my audition, and Randy, who had been one of Lee Strasberg's protégés, had been working with me on my audition pieces all summer.

For the first part of the audition, I had to do the two monologues I had prepared in front of two senior students and one of the drama teachers. After a short deliberation between the students and the teacher, I was told that I would be moving on to the second part of the audition. This meant that I had passed the first part.

Before I left the room, Anthony (Tony) Abeson, who I consider the best acting teacher I've ever studied with, pulled me aside and told me which of the two monologues I should use in the next part of the audition. I had written one of the monologues, and the other was a speech for a male character from Terrence McNally's *And Things That Go Bump in the Night*. Tony told me to do the McNally monologue for the second part of my audition. The one I had written about a kid who hated school was a first-person rant to be sure and not very good.

The next part of the audition took place in the theater of the school, in front of a panel of seniors, the head of the drama department, and a couple of teachers. I was among eight to ten people auditioning. As a group we played several different theater games and did improvisations, and then one at a time we performed our monologues. After my audition, Randy and I went back to our hotel. I was relieved that the long, stressful day was over, but I had no idea how I had done. I anxiously awaited the phone call to tell me if I had been accepted or not.

A couple of hours later, the phone rang in my hotel room. It was Abeson, who said to me, with what I would come to know as his very dry sense of humor, "In the midst of our confusion, we've decided to accept you."

I nearly fell out of my chair. I couldn't believe I had really been accepted to Performing Arts. I was ecstatic. Randy and I started jumping up and down on the beds, and then later celebrated by ordering cheeseburgers and milkshakes from room service. I had set a goal and achieved it, a first for me. Four years later, I got into NYU's drama department with that same monologue, though I ended up going to the film school instead. Not long after that, Randy was killed in a tragic motorcycle accident.

A week later, I arrived in New York ready to start high school. I thought I would immediately fit in and be happy at PA. But sometime in my first week, a rumor started that I was only accepted because my mom had bought new video equipment for the school. In fact, even before I heard about the video equipment rumor, I was really surprised by how many people were curious about my mom and dad and constantly asking me if it

51

was true that Sonny and Cher were my parents. This had never happened to me before at my LA private schools, and it had never occurred to me, especially at PA where we were all supposed to be serious artists, that anybody would care about something as trivial as who my parents were. Then somebody told me about the rumor and I was completely mortified. Here I was at my dream school and I felt again like an outsider. Luckily, that feeling didn't last long. The hoopla over my parents and the rumor about my acceptance into the school eventually went away. I fit in and made lifelong friends. PA met my expectations and ended up exceeding them. The four years that I spent there would turn out to be some of the happiest of my life.

When I moved to New York, my mom stayed back in LA to work. She was still trying to develop her acting career and money was tight, so she asked Anna Strasberg, Lee Strasberg's widow, if I could live in her apartment with her two sons Adam and David. My mom and Anna had met when my mom had talked to Lee about studying acting with him, something that never happened before he died.

Though I enjoyed the time I spent with the boys, Anna and I often butted heads. She was a sweet and nurturing woman, but, like my mom, she was always pushing me to be more feminine. I know she believed that she was doing the right thing and trying to help me fit in, but it was difficult to listen to. She was always encouraging me to grow my hair, which was short, and to dress differently, no doubt more femininely. She even had a problem with my friends who dressed kind of androgynously.

I used to call Joan once in a while because I would get so discouraged, and she would tell me to just be myself and not let Anna get me down.

It is sad to me that though things have changed since I was a kid, we still send the message to children and teens that something is wrong with you if you are different. With the proportionately higher suicide rate among GLBT youth and rampant bullying, sending these types of messages can have dire consequences.

It may seem strange to some that I moved across the country from my parents when I was just fourteen, but for me it really worked. By that time I was fiercely independent and pretty self-sufficient. I had almost total freedom to move around the city and make my own schedule. Since I was such a good kid, my parents completely trusted me to behave well, and I did.

My friends at school all seemed to have a lot of freedom—our parents were products of the sixties and all seemed to work in the arts. We were good kids, and even though there was some drinking, no one in my group ever got carried away. This was the mid-1980s; the punk scene was big, as was the Rude Boy and Mod scenes. My friends and I were heavily influenced by these scenes, dressing quite androgynously and looking like Jon Cryer's character in *Pretty in Pink*, wearing Doc Martens, Creepers, and shopping at Trash and Vaudeville, Ninety Nine X, and other thrift shops. This weird, masculine-edged, tailored style suited me perfectly.

At PA I felt more comfortable than I ever had for many reasons—the most important was that for the first time in my life I had really good friends at school. I have realized since that I'm the kind of person who really likes to belong to a group or community of people who share strong binding values. (This would prove true again and again in my life. I enjoy the camara- derie of working toward a common or personal goal in a com- munal setting, and I experienced this in the gay and lesbian community, in recovery support groups that I've been a part of, and most recently in the trans community.)

Being in the drama department at PA was the first time I felt this sense of community. Every one of my classmates loved act- ing and was dedicated to its craft. At that point I think we wanted to be professional actors when we grew up, and we all certainly wanted to improve our skills during high school. Now, almost twenty-five years later and with the help of Facebook, I am in touch with at least half of my class.

At PA I was out as a lesbian, though I didn't go shouting my sexual orientation through the halls or anything. All of my close friends knew and accepted me at face value. I did not have any other gay friends, but at least I didn't feel the need to be secretive about my sexual orientation. It was not something I hid from anyone. My friends didn't have any problem with it, so I experi- enced total acceptance.

Academics were not the focus at PA, which added to my comfort level, as well. Half our day was taken up with drama classes and other classes related to our major, such as voice and diction, stage makeup, and dance classes. The other half of the day was spent in regular academic subjects; however, at PA you could still feel successful as a student even if you got fair grades. Though two of my friends ended up as the valedictorian and salutatorian of my graduating class, most of my friends, like me, were just trying to get through our academic courses so we could graduate. And that was okay, too.

Then, in the middle of my junior year in high school, my mom moved to New York. She, too, had fallen in love with the city when we'd come two years earlier so she could act on stage, and she was finally able to relocate. Elijah was almost ten years old then, and since he didn't like the city, he had opted to go to boarding school. Suddenly my mom and I were living together, alone under the same roof for the first time ever.

My mom was dating Tom Cruise during that time, and when he went off to do a movie, he sublet his apartment in the Village to us until we found our own place. Tom had not yet begun renovating the double-loft space when we moved in, so we lived in two very large studio apartments connected by a door. My mom used one for her bedroom and I slept on a pullout couch in the other one, which we used as a living room and kitchen.

It was a relief to have a home again instead of being a visitor. And though I had begun to love my freedom, it always felt a little odd to have no adult really caring for me—I was only sixteen after all. After living with Anna Strasberg, I had moved in with my friend Orfeh and her mom, and there I'd had to sleep on the floor, buy my own groceries, make all my own meals—it wasn't easy. So when my mom came to New York, I was relieved.

In LA, there were cooks, assistants, and nannies. In New York, life for me and my mom was very stripped down and simple. In a strange way I think living in New York gave my mom as much of a sense of freedom as it did me. Nobody seemed to bother her there; there were no paparazzi in the city back then, and my mom could just do regular things like go food shopping or to the dry cleaners. Looking back on it now, I can see that this was a really special time that my mom and I had together. Everything seemed kind of normal—as if my mom could've been any working mom, it just happened that her work involved making movies.

We didn't stay at Tom's apartment very long. After that, we stayed at the Morgan Hotel and then at the apartment of Paul Stanley, a friend of my family, and then eventually, right before my senior year, my mom bought a small two-bedroom apartment close to my school and near Lincoln Center. I loved being so close to school that I could walk. That apartment became the main hangout for my friends. To this day, my mom laughs about how we'd all come over after school and clear out her recently stocked refrigerator, emptying it in a matter of minutes.

And even though my mom and I were living together, I still had a lot of freedom. In many ways, my mom was always really cool about letting me do my own thing.

But as always there was some tension, too. She made it perfectly clear that she didn't like how I looked or dressed. "You walk like a truck driver." "You dress like a slob." I heard again and again how she thought I was too masculine.

Then there was the added complication of my lie of omission—I hadn't come out to her, and I wasn't planning on doing so anytime soon. Living in such close quarters with my mom without being honest created stress. At some point I knew I was going to have to tell her that I was gay, but I was in no hurry.

I had already come out to my grandmother before I started

high school, and she didn't seem fazed or surprised by my news. My grandmother never judged me in any way; she was always loving and accepting of me and wouldn't reject me for being gay. I then told my aunt Gee a couple of years later, during my junior year. I hadn't told her earlier because I didn't want to put her in an uncomfortable position with my mom, to whom she was very close. When I finally did tell Gee, I did so because I was totally heartsick over a girl and I really needed an adult family member with whom I could talk about my feelings. I always was very close to Gee, and she was often more approachable than my mom—especially when it came to my being gay. Everyone else but my parents knew the truth about me at this point; but no one wanted to be the messenger here.

We all knew implicitly that my mom, who had plenty of gay friends, was not happy about me being so masculine. At the time, I thought the reason for my masculinity was that I was gay, and I made the assumption (as did everyone else) that my mom was going to be very disapproving of my being a lesbian. We had an unspoken understanding that all hell would break loose when she did finally discover that I was gay.

Luckily, it wasn't very difficult to keep this information from her. She was busy, and between school and friends, I, too, had a lot going on. I felt no pressure to come clean to her. I was too young and too naïve to realize that not coming out to my mother said something about my confidence in myself and my relationship with her. Unwittingly, I was walking a careful tightrope: everything was fine, unless something triggered any tension or disagreement between me and my mother.

Then I fell hard for a girl in my class, Julie. She was five foot three, with a really beautiful body. She had green eyes and long brown hair. Her family was Jewish, and she was very smart and very driven. I thought that she was extremely cute and very sexy, and for a sixteen-year-old she really was. But our relationship was problematic from the start, and in one essential way: Julie was straight. I was very into her, and she was definitely attracted to me—but she felt so uncomfortable with the idea that she might be a lesbian (or bisexual) that after we'd make out at the end of a party, she'd go out with a guy the next night. Her back-and-forth ambivalence and indecision hurt like hell.

It was a bad cycle, and one that, unfortunately, I participated in. It wreaked havoc on my ego and self-esteem to be so attached to a woman who didn't know what she wanted.

One night Julie and I were on a date and went out dancing to the China Club. When we left the club, we were both anxious to go back to my apartment.

We quietly entered the apartment, making sure the coast was clear and my mom was asleep. Slowly, we made our way to the couch, kissing as we threw off the cushions and pulled out the bed. With our clothes still on, Julie and I began making out. Suddenly the bedroom door opened and my mom came into the room on her way to kitchen. She probably could not see us from the way the couch was positioned, but like two idiots, Julie and I jumped to our feet. My mother just stared at us for a second and then walked back into her room without a word.

In the morning my mother said nothing about what she did or did not see. I learned later that she had asked Julie what had been going on. Julie simply told her that we'd fallen asleep on the couch and that she'd startled us. Mom asking Julie about what happened was quite typical of my family dynamic. We all avoid confrontation, and this was my mom's way of not having to look me in the eye and ask me an uncomfortable question. But after that night something definitely changed. My mom now had a clear distaste for Julie, and the tension between us became thicker and more tangible. My lie of omission was now more present and I began to feel uncomfortable at home.

My seventeenth birthday was a week later. I had planned my own party at a downtown restaurant. My mother ended up not coming. What followed was a few stressful months. My mom and I avoided talking about the Julie incident and what it meant: I was gay and my mother was not at all happy about it.

Though we didn't always get along, and went through a lot of the typical mother-child teenage angst, I must say that this period with Mom—even with her walking in on Julie and me— was special. In fact, I am really grateful that there was time, right before I became an adult, for us to be alone together. It was also the only time in my life up to that point when my mom wasn't involved in a serious relationship, only casually dating, so it was really just the two of us, most of the time, living our lives together.

I'm sure that it must have been hard for my mom to have a child who was so different from herself and from the way our society says young women should be. For me it was difficult to know that there was an innate part of who I was that seemed to displease my mom so much.

I always had a sense, years before I realized I was transgender, that it was never really my sexual orientation, but rather my innate masculinity, that bothered my mom. In fact I believe in most cases of homophobia, what people react violently toward is individuals not fitting into the assigned gender role that society deems fit or acceptable.

Most people don't have to come out twice in their lives. Lucky me. But now, looking back, it seems as though that first coming out was really just a foreshadowing of things to come much later.

CHAPTER FOUR

Coming Out to My Parents

When I first came out to anyone, I was thirteen, a baby. I had no sense of the gay community or even where to look for one. Gay politics were in a nascent stage and there was very little mainstream acceptance. It wasn't until I was seventeen, between my junior and senior years of high school, that I finally had a sense of the larger community to which I belonged.

I had stayed in New York that summer, wanting to hang out with my friends from school. I didn't want to go back to California with my mom, as I had done every other summer, so I rented a room from a friend of a family friend who lived in a brownstone in the West Village. My mom hadn't yet bought the apartment near my school.

My housemate was nice but kind of odd—a nudist, I think, given her habit of walking around naked—but she didn't have the kind of body that made her nudity enjoyable. My mother was back in Los Angeles by then, and then left for Boston at the end of the summer, to start working on the film *The Witches of Eastwick*. During my senior year of high school, my mom had roles in three major films—*Witches of Eastwick*, *Suspect*, and *Moonstruck*.

One beautiful Sunday in June, just after school let out, I was riding my bike around Central Park. Upon exiting the park on upper Fifth Avenue, I ran right into a parade. As I got closer, I realized that everyone in the parade was gay—I had indeed run straight into New York City's famous Gay Pride Parade! I was blown away. I had probably seen a small version of Gay Pride in LA when I was younger—a little blip that hadn't even registered—but that was nothing compared to this spectacular scene in front of me now.

Riding my bike downtown alongside the parade, I felt pumped up: there was an instant sense of belonging. This was momentous for me. Though I had support from my peers, I had no sense as yet of belonging to anything larger than myself. Yes, I knew there were other gay adults in the world, but I felt like I was the only gay teenager. The parade also made me realize that there was more to being gay then just going to bars. As hard as it may be to believe, I literally hadn't known that there was a gay movement, or gay politics, or gay leaders until that day. Up until this point, my view of the gay community was so very narrow. Watching the parade, I saw people marching for different groups and organizations and centers, and I began to see that you didn't have to be in a dark bar in order to express who you really are. You didn't have to hide. It was a very liberating experience, and the whole ride down to the Village felt almost surreal to me, with everyone celebrating who they were—out, proud, and happy. It was a revelation.

Remember, this was the eighties, before the Internet, multiple out gay characters on television, and organized GLBT youth groups across the country. Seeing this enormous parade made a sudden and huge difference in my life from that point on. I gained a sense of community in life outside high school. I finally fit in somewhere in the larger world. I was not so alien, so different after all.

Unfortunately, I wasn't quite ready to be a part of this massive community I had found. Back in my own world, I had been telling my friends that I was gay, and no one was fazed. However, sometimes when I did come out to someone new, that person would ask me if I'd ever tried having sex with a man. When I would answer no, they'd sometimes say to me, "How do you know that you're a lesbian if you've never had sex with a man?"

I started to become so frustrated with people asking me this ridiculous question that I decided to give in. I decided that I would have sex with a man so I would never have to hear that question again. And though logically I didn't think it would change my attraction toward women, I guess something in me wanted to make sure. Ironically, given who my peers were, the one and only man that I ever had sex with in my life was a Marine. It might seem strange, but it makes perfect sense to me. For one thing he was willing and safe. I had known Rick for a while, and he knew that I liked women and was just experimenting. In fact, I knew him through a woman, Audrey, who I had been seeing.

If I truly unpack this situation, I know there was more to my choice. I've always had a strange fascination with the military and anything to do with the armed forces. I collected knives all through my childhood and most of my adulthood. I've always been interested in weapons—knives, swords, and guns—and am drawn to all things that denote masculinity—boxing, mixed martial arts, football. I'm not a violent person at all, but I find myself really attracted to these examples of hypermasculinity. I liked the tough-guy, hypermasculine identity of a Marine, which is, if I am honest, another reason why Rick appealed to me.

After it was all over, I remember being surprised by what a non-event it was. I thought having sex with a man would make me feel something, that it would be disgusting or traumatic or maybe even, though I doubted it, really amazing. But it was just sex with a partner whose gender I wasn't attracted to, and it left me feeling kind of flat.

So even though I was coming into my own in terms of my sexual orientation, I still felt some kind of societal pressure to be "normal." Later that summer, I was in Palm Springs visiting my dad and I met the son of the bookkeeper for my dad's restaurant. We immediately hit it off and seemed to have a lot in common. He ended up asking me out on a lunch date, and I accepted his invitation. Unfortunately, I can't remember the kid's name, but I remember that he was an art student home from college. He seemed intelligent and interesting—a nice-looking guy with shoulder-length hair and an artsy/hippie kind of vibe. I remember thinking at the time that if it was possible for me to be interested in a guy romantically, it would be somebody like him. We went to lunch at a local Mexican restaurant and then to see the movie *About Last Night*, with Rob Lowe and Demi Moore. All through the movie I sat there thinking about my ex-girlfriend Julie, who I was still in love with. . . . And it was completely clear to me at that moment that I just wasn't sexually attracted to men.

I see this time in my life as one of experimenting. Like most teenagers, I was exploring myself and my options in a fairly mindless way. I thought these encounters with men led to only one conclusion: I must really be a lesbian. But my need to experiment at all perhaps speaks to the idea that my lesbian identity was not quite right, either. Looking back and digging deep, I actually think that this interest in men was not about sex, but about my unconscious desire to be a man. My attraction to the art student was not about wanting to be *with* him, but wanting to be *like* him. What I now understand is that heterosexual men have attractions or connections to other men that are completely nonsexual in nature. Bromances are commonplace—Hollywood even makes movies about them. But these relationships between men are real. As a teen I occasionally found myself having deeper or more intense feelings for a man; maybe we had a lot in common, or I just thought he was really cool, or handsome, or smart. And still believing that I was female, I assumed my feelings must be of a romantic nature. Now I know they were not. The few times that this happened to me it was really confusing. Now it all makes sense.

Around that time, I ran into a guy from Walden, the school I'd attended briefly in New York when my mom did the play. I was fascinated by him. He was now an actor on Broadway and seemed utterly cool.

Trying to get his attention, I asked him if he wanted to get together and hang out after one of his matinee performances. I then proceeded to dress up in a very feminine outfit, put on makeup, do my hair—thinking that was what I was supposed to do and that, again, my feelings for him were romantic. But once on the date, I felt completely out of sorts. What was I doing? What was my attraction to this guy all about? Wasn't I gay? If so, why was I attracted to a man? I felt uncomfortable dressing in such a feminine manner, but I thought that was what men liked.

When confronted with the possibility of a sexual encounter, it was clear to me that that's not what I wanted from this friend. If I had the ability to really analyze the situation at the time, I might have been able to understand that I was attracted to the fact that he was a working actor and an interesting, intelligent, and handsome guy. Again, what I wanted was to be like him, not to be with him.

This kind of disconnect also occurred when I was studying acting. I loved acting, but when I was playing a female role, it felt completely uncomfortable and awkward. The acting curriculum the first two years at PA had been all about playing roles close to who we were. My school taught students to act from an internal, personally emotional place. We were asked to be authentic within our characters, from moment to moment, and not take big leaps into playing characters that were too different from ourselves.

But even when I did a scene in which I was playing a lesbian character, I felt ill at ease. As odd as it sounds, the role felt like too much of a stretch. The scene was from the teen book *Happy Endings Are All Alike*, about two high school girls having a budding romance. They'd meet in the woods to be together, kiss, and you get the picture. I don't clearly remember everything about the story line, but the essential premise should have been easy for me. What better role for me than a lesbian high school student? And yet I remember feeling like I couldn't embody the character at all.

Even my love of acting couldn't get me past this awkwardness. I was a lesbian. Why was acting the role so strange? If only I could have understood that I was transgender back then, I could have saved myself years of pain and confusion.

It wasn't until my senior year, when I did the witches' scene from *Macbeth*, that I truly felt like I was doing good work. My two scene partners and I decided to base our characters on animals. We started the scene before any dialogue was spoken. I was a gorilla, and then morphed into humanoid form to speak the lines. I played my witch character completely genderless, with the air of an angry territorial ape, and for the first time I felt perfectly comfortable on stage.

The Spring Drama Festival was the only time in four years that you actually got to perform in front of a real audience, not just your teachers and peers. It was a big deal. The festival consisted of four different plays done by different directors, with each play performed multiple times over two weekends. I was cast in *A Midsummer Night's Dream* directed by James Moody, a working actor who often taught at my school. I played the male character Peter Quince. In the play, there is a group of laborers, usually referred to as the rustics, who decide to perform a play for the duke's wedding reception. Peter Quince is the rustic who organizes the production—the director of the play within the play.

I nailed that part, too. Playing Peter Quince felt like what I thought acting should feel like. I felt comfortable and real on stage though I was clearly playing a character that wasn't like me. As any actor does, I made certain choices about how to approach the character, deciding to play him as an older man, in his fifties or sixties, with a somewhat stiff physical demeanor and a slightly stuffy or conceited way about him. I aged and bearded my face with stage makeup and wore a large fake stomach under my sacklike toga in order to conceal the fact that I had breasts. This character was probably the one the least like me that I had ever portrayed, and yet the simple fact that he was male completely eradicated that strange, uncomfortable, out-of-place feeling that I felt whenever I was portraying a female character.

The one thing that was a little uncomfortable about playing Peter Quince in the Spring Drama Festival was that this was the first time my parents were going to get to see me perform since I'd started at PA. And they were going to have to watch their daughter play a man.

My dad and stepmom, Mary, flew to New York City from Palm Springs for the show. I was so excited to see them and happy that they got to see me perform. If either Mary or my dad thought it was odd that I was playing a man, neither showed it. Both were supportive and seemed proud of me.

My mom came to the play on closing night, the Saturday before Mother's Day. I was incredibly nervous about her seeing me on stage playing a man. I knew she would probably hate seeing me so overtly male. She had been making it clear for years that she wished I would act more like a girl, and here I was up on stage in full male drag and quite convincingly pulling it off. Maybe in some remote crevice of my being, I knew that I was being my true self on that stage, and that my mom wasn't ready for that reality. It turned out that I wasn't ready for that reality, either.

After the show, everything seemed normal and my mom did her best to seem proud of my performance. My mom is not the kind of person who gushes over every small accomplishment. She's critical about her own work and holds others to her standards. The good thing about that is that when my mom says she likes something or that she is proud, you know she really means it. The difficult thing is that if she doesn't understand something, disapproves, or isn't impressed, you are bound to figure that out, too.

My mom was polite and supportive and told me that I'd done a good job. Then she left, and I went to celebrate the end of the Spring Drama Festival with the rest of the department, getting drunk and hanging out on a giant rock in Central Park, as Performing Arts drama students had been doing for years. I was relieved when my mom was gone; I knew she wouldn't ever bring that night up to me again. We could just sweep Peter Quince under the rug.

I had been accepted into NYU film school for the fall, and after graduation, I took off with my friend Shula to Europe for six weeks, a trip that was a graduation present from my mom. It was the first vacation that I had ever taken without my parents, and traveling around Europe with a peer made me feel really grown-up. Shula and I started the trip with a few days in St. Tropez with my mom and brother and family friends, and then we were off on our own to Venice. I have to admit that at this time I experienced my first ever "poor little rich kid" moment going from the best hotel in St. Tropez to one step above a youth hostel in Venice, Italy, but I quickly regained my composure. I had big plans for my first adventure out of the country away from my parents. I was going to meet other young lesbians and hook up. However, once the trip started, I realized I had no idea how to go about meeting other lesbians and I was terrified to ask anyone where the local gay watering holes might be. Shula, newly single, had no problem meeting eligible young foreign men, but the closest I got to any action was when a guy who worked at the Moulin Rouge in Paris offered me a job as a topless dancer, no doubt because of the size of my double-D breasts.

After Europe, I spent the rest of the summer hanging out in Palm Springs. My stepmother, Mary, taught me how to drive and I got my driver's license. I also began to think about coming out to my dad. He and I had always been close, and our relationship meant a lot to me. He still seemed to accept me for who I was, much as he had when I was a child. Unlike my mother, he did not judge the way I dressed or carried myself, and I always felt like I could be myself with him. And because we were so close, I felt a bit more pressure to come out to him. I felt like he should know the truth—especially when others in my family already did. But I was still scared that if he had a negative reaction to my being gay, I might lose our camaraderie. It was a big risk.

While staying at his house that summer, I did a bit of fishing around, trying to discover if my dad knew I was gay. I remember hoping that my father would bring up the subject so I didn't have to. When this didn't seem to work, I began to give him direct hints: I left a lesbian romance novel lying by my bed. I brought up anything in the news that was relevant to gay rights. I also began asking him questions like "Is there anything I could tell you about myself that would make you not love me anymore?" He didn't take the bait.

That summer, I ended up kissing Joan for the first time, right before heading back to New York to start college. She had invited me to a party that a friend of hers was having near her house in

Studio City. I remember being very excited about going to my first lesbian party. I don't know what I expected it to be like exactly, but I did imagine that I would meet other young lesbians and that I would instantly feel comfortable, as if I really belonged. When I got to the party, reality crushed my fantasy.

I was a good fifteen years younger than anybody there, and knowing only one or two people, I felt anxious and uncomfortable. Somehow, I settled in after a while and had a nice time hanging out with Joan and meeting some more of her acquaintances. Because I'd had a little too much to drink, it was decided (by Joan and her then-girlfriend) that I would spend the night at Joan's house, which was only a few blocks away.

But on the way from the party to her house, Joan and I started to make out in her car, which for me was like living out a fantasy that I'd had since I was thirteen years old. Joan was such a feminine woman that kissing her made me feel very masculine. I seemed to know intuitively that she wanted her partner to be sexually in control and to take charge in a more typically male or masculine way, and I found myself comfortable in that role.

After that night, nothing much happened between Joan and me. We reverted to being friends as I went off to begin college.

Back in New York, toward the end of my senior year, my mom had sold the apartment on the Upper West Side and bought a place downtown. We had a very cool triplex on East 4th Street above the old Tower Records store (sadly, closed now), looking over the East River from the floor-to-ceiling windows and a wraparound deck on the third floor. My mom's room, the living room, and the kitchen were all on the second floor. Elijah's and my bedrooms were on the first floor. (Elijah was still at boarding school and came home on weekends and holidays. He was only eleven years old, so I wasn't out to him yet.) Keith Richards was our neighbor. I can remember being able to look east and see a friend of mine who lived on 3rd Street between Avenues A and B—we could wave at each other from our apartments—that's how clear the view was.

Early in the fall, my dad and his wife, Mary, came to visit. We went to Smith & Wollensky's steak house, my family's favorite. When I accompanied my dad and Mary back to their hotel, my dad not so casually turned to Mary and said he and I were going to have coffee alone in the hotel lounge.

After a few minutes of small talk, my dad said, "Chas, do you want to talk about anything? Do you have anything you want to tell me? It's okay—I won't be upset."

We looked at each other knowingly.

After hesitating for a minute, I finally said, "I'm gay."

I quickly explained that I had wanted to tell him for a long time, but I was afraid that it would come between us.

"I've got to tell you, Chas, that I've suspected for a while. You need to know that, no matter what, I love you."

A huge weight lifted off my shoulders. I immediately felt even more comfortable around him because I didn't need to hide anything anymore. No more changing girls' names to boys'. No more being purposefully vague about what I was doing and with whom.

We didn't discuss the fact that my mom didn't yet know. My dad was aware of my relationship with her, and I think he understood why I was in no hurry to come out to her.

I still didn't have the guts to tell my mom. I would tell myself she was too busy and distracted by her work, that she didn't want to know anyway. I knew she was going to freak out. I was afraid to tell her. Period. I just couldn't handle the idea of my mother being upset with me. Even though she rarely lost her cool, I had an irrational fear of my mom being disappointed or angry with me. She had never punished me or raised her voice at me. If anything she reacted too coolly or distantly if she was upset. But I was terrified of displeasing her. I told myself that I needed time to figure myself out more.

Then life intervened.

Near the end of the first semester of my freshman year, I met Heidi. We got involved fast and furiously in that no-holds-barred lesbian way. Heidi was tall and skinny, with a perm of blond hair and a stunning face. When she was interested or passionate about something, she had a way of conveying that excitement so that it was palpable. If she was explaining something new, something that I didn't know about, I felt like I was listening to a lecture given by the coolest professor on campus.

I was still living at the apartment on East 4th Street. My mom had returned to LA for a movie, but Rob, her boyfriend at the time, was still in New York, so we shared the apartment. I'd become a bit more brazen because I'd come out to my dad and because my mom wasn't around. One morning after Heidi had spent the night, Rob knocked on my door just as I was waking up.

"Chas, you've got to call your mom. She talked to your dad and she knows what's going on."

It was really early in the morning, and even earlier in LA—and Rob looked exhausted—as if he'd been up all night on the phone with my mother. Shit. Absolute terror set in.

My hands went clammy, my heart started to pound in my chest. I felt like I was going to throw up.

My worst nightmare had come true—the moment I'd been avoiding for the past five years had arrived and it wasn't under my control.

So I called my mother.

"Mom, it's me."

She didn't wait: "Why didn't you tell me what was going on? How could you do this to me? I had to find out from your father!" She was furious. I didn't say much. I tried to explain. But she was just pissed. She launched into a tirade about how everyone had known except her and she felt like an idiot. I could tell she was also really, really hurt.

My mother works hard and doesn't like drama in her life. Now she was beside herself and I had caused it. The sweet little girl who didn't like to make waves had enraged her mother. I was horrified. Ashamed. You name it.

I tried to explain that I was glad she finally knew the truth. "I think it will make us closer, Mom," I tried.

She only said, "No, this will push us apart. I want you to get out of the apartment now."

And she hung up.

I was devastated and in shock. Heidi helped me pack up my stuff, and like a robot I followed her over to the apartment she shared with Amy, her roommate.

After a week my mom called to say she was sorry that she'd

gotten so upset, and she asked me to come to LA so we could talk. She also wanted to meet Heidi. By the time Heidi and I got on the plane, I was feeling apprehensive but relieved. My mother finally knew the truth; I didn't have to hide anything from her anymore. But I knew coming home was going to feel awkward. After all that time of holding the truth inside, I wasn't sure how things were going to play out now that everything was out in the open.

When we arrived at the house in Benedict Canyon, my mom had clearly calmed down. I believe that she had discussed the situation with her therapist and begun to process why she'd lashed out. She was upset that she'd been the last one in the family to find out I was gay. She had suspected but wanted confirmation and really resented having to hear that from my father. She told me that when she called my dad, he kind of rubbed in the fact that I'd told him first.

All I could see on her face was her genuine disappointment that her "baby girl" was gay.

We sat around her house and had lunch. I caught up on the family and we began to adjust to each other in a new way. My mom didn't know what to make of Heidi that first meeting. On the one hand she was smart, attractive, thin, and fairly feminine, all attributes my mom prizes. However, Heidi was also a bit confrontational, which seemed to make my mom uncomfortable.

The next day, I accompanied my mother to therapy. I don't quite remember what we talked about. I do recall trying to convince my mom that I was happy being gay and that she would be happy about it, too, once she got used to the fact.

Our therapy session wasn't life-changing, but it was the first honest conversation we'd had about my sexual orientation. Being with a therapist enabled us to have a safe place to talk. And my mom did turn around very quickly. Her initial reaction was strong, but she quickly adjusted to reality. It certainly was a great improvement from "I want you to get out of the apartment now."

I can't say my mother fully accepted my sexual orientation after one short week. Over the next few months and years my mother gradually became very comfortable. But at the time, as it is for so many members of the GLBT community, coming out to my parents was difficult and scary. Fear of rejection and disappointment loomed over me—for very different reasons. In my father's case I was afraid of losing the close, nonjudgmental relationship that we had always shared. My mother, on the other hand, had always made it perfectly clear that the thing about me that was "different" was not desirable to her. I know now that her being the last in the family to know about my sexual orientation only made matters more difficult.

In many ways this was the beginning of my adult relationship with my mother. The fact that I could now be honest about my sexuality did bring us closer. When I was writing *Family Outing*, she told me that she had suspected that I was gay since I was a little kid. When she did finally confront me, some part of her knew she was ready to know—she just had to face it.

Now I was out to both my parents, and once all was said and done, I felt a huge sense of relief.

Looking back at my coming out experience in 1987, I now know it was only part of the story. I was never a lesbian. I confused my male gender identity with my sexual orientation. Because I was attracted to women and didn't understand what it meant to be transgender, I concluded that I must be gay. I wish that I'd known then what I know now and that I'd only had to come out once to my parents, but that's not how my journey played out. I am a strong believer in the idea that things happen for a reason, usually to help us grow and become better people.

The relief that I felt coming out to my parents of course didn't last. When I was thirty-one I started to understand that I was really a transgender man. This discovery landed me back in the closet for another nine years. Of course, I never had the opportunity to come out to my dad about being transgender. People ask me all the time what I think my father would have thought about me transitioning. The truth is I have no idea. I'd like to think that he would've been totally supportive, but I also know that he was of a different, more conservative generation and might not have understood. Regardless of what his reaction would have been, I really wish he was alive today to see the happy and confident man I've become. I slayed a lot of demons to get here, and I can't help but imagine that he would be proud of me.

CHAPTER FIVE

Our Band

Heidi and I officially moved in together as soon as we could. I was so in love with her that I couldn't quite think straight, and I was also the type of lesbian to move in on the second date, a habit that, regardless of my gender, took many years to outgrow. But at eighteen years old, nothing seemed to make more sense than to move in with Heidi.

We had a blast together just doing the New York thing—going to movies, finding new restaurants to try, and playing music in her apartment. She was already an accomplished musician, playing guitar and piano. Soon after we got together, she began teaching me how to play both piano and guitar chords. We began—in a haphazard way—to sing together. It turned out that I actually had a natural voice, which I guess wasn't much of a surprise given what my parents did for a living.

Right away, Heidi seemed a bit concerned about how I presented myself as a lesbian. I didn't know this at the time, but she had received a lot of grief from her lesbian peers pressuring her to dress a certain way and act a certain way—as if there were one acceptable way to be a lesbian. She felt pressure from her peer group of lesbians when she was first coming out not to wear makeup, not to shave, not to color her hair. They were crunchy-granola-type lesbians who thought any attention to feminine style undermined you as a lesbian and feminist. But that just wasn't Heidi's natural style—gay or not. Heidi was a lipstick lesbian before anyone thought it was chic, and she created a lesbian identity that worked for her. So it was kind of ironic that she was putting some pressure on me to lose my natural masculine style. She focused on my hair first.

Let it be known that I did have quite a horrible eighties hairstyle—it was long in the back and short in the front, some kind of mullet gone awry. Changing it was probably a good idea. But changing it *for* Heidi was more indicative of who I was then. At the time, my hairstyle gave me a way to be more masculine, a part of my never-ending internal negotiation. I was always trying to find my way and feel comfortable in my skin, and having the right hair meant a lot. My hair was long and I used a lot of product to heighten the top, which I then wore in my version of a pompadour because I was obsessed with the fifties. (This began when I was a kid and used to comb back my wet hair trying to look like Fonzie from *Happy Days*). Then Heidi started dressing me—she wanted me to change my overtly masculine, butch style and adopt more of an androgynous look, like her. Heidi didn't appreciate my baggy men's suit pants and bowling shirts, either. She wanted me to wear cool jeans that were more styled, and she made it clear that my butch style and persona just didn't work for her.

At first, I wasn't that aware of or bothered by Heidi's controlling behavior—"Let's go here for dinner." "Why don't you wear this shirt?" "Don't you think you should cut your hair?" I didn't really have strong opinions either way, and it just seemed easier to go along with her and let Heidi's more assertive personality take charge of us as a couple. I simply acquiesced. But this kind of dynamic seems now to reflect again how out of touch with myself I was back then. I always seemed to look to other people to make me feel secure and grounded. I didn't realize that when I let Heidi guide how I dressed and wore my hair, let her choose our restaurants and movies, I might have done so at my own expense. Clearly, I was invested in my relationship with Heidi and wanted her to love me and accept me, which meant that I was motivated to be who she wanted me to be. This meant tamping down my natural style.

My dynamic with Heidi was part of a larger pattern that got started when I was a child and didn't want to bother my mom, dad, or Harriet. So attached to the need to please the people that I loved, I became an expert at adjusting my behavior, look, or expectations to theirs, always compromising a bit of myself for the sake of the relationship. Internally, this must have been a very delicate balance, and often hard to maintain. In my earlier relationships with some women, I had behaved in much the same way, acquiescing to pressure to be more feminine to some degree. I would say this pressure to be more feminine and less masculine was a constant through all but very few of my romantic relationships with women. But the overriding result left me feeling that there was something wrong with me.

That spring, my mom was nominated for a Best Actress Academy Award for her performance in *Moonstruck*. All of us were thrilled for her. She'd been working so hard on her craft, and it showed. Now she was being celebrated by her peers for her work. She invited me and Heidi, my brother, and her boyfriend Rob to the awards. I remember getting ready beforehand, and of course, I had to dress up. I didn't wear a dress, but something from my mother's closet instead—a pair of black leggings with a long black sequined top and black boots. My mother's friend and hairdresser Jose Eber did my hair in a mass of curls.

I didn't like the way I looked so, as usual, I just tried to ignore my reflection in the mirror and focused instead on Heidi, who was out of her mind with excitement from the whole scene. She'd bought a special dress for the occasion—a black-and-white strapless top attached to a skirt that was made up of individual poofs that circled the whole bottom half of the dress. Jose had done her hair as well, spiking it on top of her head. She loved the way she looked and was so excited about it. At that time in my life it would have never even occurred to me to wear a tuxedo to the Oscars, which is, of course, what I would do now.

Best Actress is one of the last awards to be announced, so it was a long night. But the payoff was huge: my mom won, and seeing her up on that stage was pretty fantastic. Despite my own discomfort, we had an amazing time that night. I had never realized that during the commercial breaks, everyone seated in the auditorium gets up and starts chatting and mingling. It was one giant schmoozefest.

Typical of my mom, after the ceremonies, all she wanted to do was go home and hang with us, my aunt, my grandmother, and some other very close friends. I was only nineteen and Heidi twenty-three, so naturally we were totally psyched to go to some of the famous Oscar afterparties, but I think we just went back to my mom's house and ordered pizza. In the end, I was happy to celebrate the way my mom wanted to.

By the end of my freshman year, it was clear to me that I did not want to continue at NYU. Heidi was graduating and moving on, and I didn't want to risk losing her. In the back of my head, I also didn't believe that college was so paramount to my future. After all, the only one in my family to have even graduated from high school was my aunt Gee; no one had gone to college. Nobody really cared that I quit school. Everyone in my family had become quite successful without higher education, and I think they took my decision in stride.

But there was one thing I was determined to do at the end of the school year: have breast reduction surgery. My mom supported my decision to have this surgery. As a fairly small-breasted woman, she felt genuinely sorry for me having to carry around double-D-size breasts. I had hated my breasts since they first developed, and I hoped that making them smaller would make me hate them less.

My breasts had been in my way since they first appeared, and now they made me uncomfortable, even embarrassed, during sex. I found myself mentally checking out or squirming when my breasts were touched, wanting to leave my body completely. This surgery felt like a great step toward becoming more comfortable in my body.

In June, after the NYU semester ended and Heidi graduated, we went out to LA for my procedure. The surgery itself was painful and my recovery was miserable. By the time all the swelling was gone, I was down to a 34C bra size. It was a definite improvement, but I still hated my breasts. I know now that this is a classic example of gender dysphoria, which I developed after puberty, and had I been aware of even the notion that transgender people existed, this should have been obvious evidence that I was experiencing something more than a discovery of my sexual orientation. (I actually know another trans-guy who had a breast reduction years before transitioning or realizing he was transgender.) In the end, though my breast reduction did offer a little relief, it was short-lived. I was disappointed that the surgeon could not make them smaller, and I still felt that whether large or small, breasts did not belong on my body.

When I had healed enough to travel, my family headed off to St. Tropez for our annual summer vacation. I was totally psyched to be going back to Europe and was thrilled to have Heidi join us. We met up with my mom, my mother's good friend Paulette, Michelle Pfeiffer, my brother, his best friend Balthazar Getty, and Rob, my mom's boyfriend. We all stayed at the Byblos Hotel, my mom's favorite hotel in that area, and where I had stayed the year before with Shula.

After about a week with the family, Heidi and I were ready to go off on our own. Heidi had never been to Europe, and I was thrilled to be the one to lead the tour. Our first stop was Paris, then Amsterdam, and then London. All through the trip, I kept thinking about how good I felt just being with Heidi.

Though we were totally enjoying ourselves as we traveled by train from city to European city, the stress about what we were going to do once we returned home began to mount. Now that she had graduated, Heidi felt a lot of pressure to figure out what she was supposed to do for a career. And since I was going to drop out, I felt equally stressed about my own plans.

"What the hell are we going to do?" we'd ask each other as we boarded another train. Heidi thought she was going to go into film or television production (she'd gotten a film degree at NYU), and I had basically not a clue.

Every city we visited, we came up with a new idea: "Let's move to Paris and sell antiques!" "Let's open a hash bar in Amsterdam!" "Let's run a pub in London!" We were literally all over the map.

Then one summer night in Paris, as we were crossing the Pont Neuf bridge, with the Seine and Notre Dame in the background, I blurted out what had really been circling inside of my head: "I think we should make music together!"

For a while I had been thinking that I should try to have a career as a singer-songwriter. I did not have a great passion for music or singing, or even songwriting; but Heidi and I had always had fun when we were playing music in our apartment. I was beginning to become more confident writing songs, and I knew that I had a nice voice—a bit like my mom's. But more than that, I had absolutely *no* idea what else to do with my life. Embarking on a new career just because you can't think of anything else to do is not all that inspiring, so collaborating with Heidi seemed like a stroke of genius. Being madly in love with her helped, and any activity that we could do together seemed better than having to do something alone.

Heidi's passion about music was just the push we needed. She absolutely loved music, knew more about the history of rock 'n' roll than anybody I knew, and was a great playwright, a skill, I was convinced, would surely translate to song lyrics.

After our summer trip to Europe, we returned to New York and went right to work figuring out what we needed to do to make a record and become famous rock stars. When I'm motivated, I'm motivated, and creating music was no different. I became focused in the way I had been about getting accepted to PA for high school.

You would have thought I might have gone to my parents for advice, but I was very used to being independent and wanted to accomplish my goals on my own merit. This was true of getting into PA, NYU, and now our hopeful recording career. When you grow up in Hollywood and have celebrities as parents, you never want to be accused of enjoying the benefits of nepotism, or at least I didn't. I probably took this to an extreme in my life. I had gleaned from my mom an incredible work ethic that focused on one thing: you have to fight for everything. I knew this was true for her as a child when she was put in the position by my grandmother of taking care of her little sister, and it was true again after she and my father divorced, she split from Gregg Allman, and she was left to raise two small kids.

Like her, I expected to work hard for things, and it never entered my mind to ask my mother—or my father for that matter—for help. I don't think I even played them any of our early music. Honestly, I don't think that it's all that surprising that I didn't go to my parents about my music. I mean, what teen wants their parents' advice about anything? As I've aged, my stubborn pride has lessened, though to be honest, I do still prefer to take care of myself, without help from my mom.

Both Heidi and I were young, idealistic, and pigheaded. And, of course, we knew next to nothing about the difference between making music and forging a career in music. Immediately, taking even the first few steps was daunting. It's one thing to play some acoustic guitar in your own living room, strumming away to Crosby Stills & Nash; it's an entirely different undertaking to accomplish all that goes into writing music and recording it. We were highly influenced by the big bands from the sixties and seventies—the Beatles, Fleetwood Mac, the Mamas and the Papas, and the Beach Boys. We didn't have a definite sound, and we were testing ourselves and trying to find our groove.

We ended up getting a lot of advice from my friend Orfeh's boyfriend. Mike was already a professional musician, and he and Orfeh were starting to make music together, too. They had a home studio and were making demos. It was Mike who told us what equipment to buy and how to get started. With some money that I'd earned from my appearances on *The Sonny and Cher Comedy Hour* as a child, we bought a four-track recorder, a guitar, a drum machine, a keyboard, and other essentials to write music and record demos.

Then we got our first break.

Heidi was a total Dead Head, and my mom's manager Bill "Bumper" Sammeth had gotten us great tickets for a series of shows at Madison Square Garden. The tickets came with backstage passes, and after the show we got friendly with Bob Weir, one of the lead singers and the rhythm guitar player. Then, for New Year's, we decided to go to a Grateful Dead concert in San Francisco. We'd made this crappy demo of three songs, and after the show Bob invited us back to his house in Marin County to play him the demo. He liked it and suggested we put a band together. I think he was being kind—he was, in fact, a really nice guy. The music itself was really bad, but he encouraged us to keep going for it.

We were green and knew next to nothing about the music business, but we took his advice and started to put a band together. Still working out of our apartment, we played, wrote songs, auditioned potential band members, and the songs began to get better. It took us several months, but we ended up choosing a drummer, bass player, guitar player, and keyboardist for our band.

For a year we played, we played, we played—in our apartment. This two year period was very exciting. Heidi and I and the band did everything together—we lived and breathed our music. We wrote songs, played, hung out, and imagined ourselves up on stage as famous rock stars. Our friends would come to our rehearsals, and then we'd all go out to eat, or back to our apartment, where we'd all stay up half the night playing poker and doing whip-its, our drug of choice then. These people became our family. We were young and energetic, New York was the place to be, and we were in its very center.

By the summer of 1990, the band was formed, and Heidi and I had completed a batch of new, well-written songs. The next step was making another demo. All of the tracks on the demo sounded good, but none of us knew how to actually mix a song. We had attempted to mix the songs ourselves, but the tracks ended up sounding muddy. I knew that Bumper was in New York at the time, so on a whim, I called him and asked if he would come over and listen to the demo and give us his advice. He came over, listened patiently, and then told us he could get someone in LA to mix it for free. I had broken my own rule of not using my parents' connections for my own goals—but in this case it seemed more than necessary.

A few weeks later, Heidi, our drummer, Alan, and I went out to LA to mix our demo. At this point, we still didn't have a name for the band. (Later, playing gigs around New York, we kept changing our name because the press would show up and write a trashy article about us. We needed the practice playing live, so anytime we got booked to play a gig we used a different name, including the Bandwagon, Vicious Rumors, and Herman and the Scrank Dogs.)

Bumper got Mark Hudson, a singer-songwriter, and Tom, an engineer who worked on my mother's records, to help us remix our demo. Mark was an old family friend and had a band with his brothers in the seventies. The Hudson Brothers also had a TV show in the seventies that was the summer replacement for my parents' show. All of us spent a day in the studio as Mark and Tom mixed our three songs. The results this time were amazing, and we were thrilled. After the demos were properly remixed— and sounding really good—Bumper said, "Why don't we share it with John Kalodner," who was then the head of A and R at Geffen Records.

We then got a meeting Kalodner and, together with Bumper, went over to the Geffen offices, thinking we might just get some good advice on what we should do next. But Kalodner liked what he heard enough to sign us for a development deal on the spot. He gave us some money and arranged for a young A and R woman in New York to mentor us for the next six months. She arranged for us to play some live gigs and got us a stylist to work on the band's look. We were blown away.

Appearance is a major aspect of the music business. Heidi had already gotten me to wear makeup for any business-related meetings, and my hair was now highlighted blond. Getting a stylist meant yet another step away from my own natural style. Jessica, our stylist, was cool and offbeat, and worked with us to develop a kind of sixties retro look that reflected our music, but it was still a much more feminine look than I was comfortable with. Jessica didn't force us to wear miniskirts and bustiers, but I still felt uncomfortable. Heidi loved our new outfits (which seemed like costumes to me), so I tried to quash my reservations and make a go of it. I was all too aware of the fact that while the outfits weren't overtly sexy, they were still women's clothes and more feminine than anything I had ever worn before.

Right before Christmas, I got a call from my mom's publicist saying that the tabloid *Star* was going to out me as a lesbian. I freaked out. I worried that Geffen wouldn't follow through on the development deal and my career would be over before it ever started.

I called my mom immediately.

"Is there anything we can do to stop them?" I asked frantically.

I was expecting a bit of an "I told you so," because she had warned me that something like this might happen. But my mom actually felt terrible for me and helped me to calm down. She was always good in a crisis.

Geffen didn't drop us, but Heidi and I now had to pretend we weren't gay. We had to act as if we were friends, both dating men, and never, ever give the paparazzi an opportunity to see us as a couple. At that time I believed with all my heart that you could not be a recording artist and be openly gay. That's what everybody thought back in 1990. I willingly started going out to public events with our guitar player Mitch as my beard, to try to refute the article.

Heidi and I had stopped going out to any gay bars, or clubs, when we first decided to do music together, but the damage was already done. I later found out that the tabloids had known for years that I was gay and were just waiting for me to do something that would classify me as a public figure, which the Geffen deal did. We became afraid that anytime we left our apartment, someone would break in while we were gone, so we got rid of any photos that showed us being the least bit affectionate. Reporters called our apartment constantly, followed us, and our daily lives became completely constricted. The tabloids also harassed Heidi's parents, calling and hanging up and staking out their house on Long Island. All of this made us feel extremely paranoid.

The tabloid hysteria went on for almost a year, and it completely wrecked my sense of privacy and safety. This was my first real experience dealing with the press in such an invasive, negative way. I felt victimized and powerless to protect myself. I was also convinced that if anyone had incriminating evidence—a photo or love letter—my budding music career would be ruined.

At the same time that Heidi and I felt pressure from the music business to stay closeted (some of which was self-imposed, I might add), the gay community was angry that I *wouldn't* come out publicly. We felt torn, boxed in, and humiliated.

For the next three years, I denied that I was gay. I lived behind closed doors and windows, convinced that if the public knew

Heidi and I were gay and a couple, our fledgling music career would be destroyed. I lived my life in an emotional and physical straitjacket that preyed on my worst fears and insecurities. This experience also drove home the challenge of being a public figure. I don't think of myself as a celebrity, but because of my parents, I am often hounded by the press, who think they can peer into my life. Consequently, most of what I do—innocuous or not—comes under public scrutiny, and I have had to adjust to that fact of my life.

My fear of the repercussions from being outed made me deny who I was. Over time, living a lie became more and more difficult. The stress of living with my blinds always closed, wondering if I was being followed and never being able to connect with my community, gnawed at me, making me feel unsafe and vulnerable, all too familiar feelings.

Of course, I was young then and still learning how to deal with my own emotional life, and I was not quite dealing with my feelings. I followed an internal mandate to be strong and resilient— taking cues from how my mother handled the stresses inherent in a life led in the public eye.

Looking back on this first run-in with the press, it's hard for me to relate to my own fear. Though I didn't realize it at the time, going through that experience actually ended up teaching me how to deal with the press, and helped to thicken my skin, so that now mean-spirited stories in the tabloids barely affect me at all—and the tabloids have only become more fierce since then.

In the end it took me five years to finally take my power back, when I told my story, my way, and came out on the cover of the *Advocate.*

CHAPTER SIX

Putting Out for
the Music Business

When I think back on my career in music, I see this: an early period of intense creativity and fun, followed by years of frustration as I tried to push myself into a mold that just did not fit. In many ways, the fact that I started my music career in the closet, pretending to be something I wasn't, says it all.

As our development deal was coming to an end, Heidi and I started to prepare to make a new three-song demo for John Kalodner so he could decide whether or not to sign us to a formal record deal. Heidi and I had been a working really hard to come up with new songs, and Tom, who had mixed our last demo, came to New York to work with our band on arrangements. We played John some recordings. John hated them. It became clear that if Tom produced our demo alone, we would never get signed to a record deal. At that point Heidi and I flew back to LA and got Mark Hudson involved again to coproduce with Tom, who happened to have a twenty-four-track recording studio at his house.

Mark brought in his own musicians to play on the demo, and they were amazing. Tom and Mark were supposed to be producing the demo together, but in truth Mark did all the heavy lifting. Heidi and I both were really blown away with Mark's talents, and amazed by how good our music now sounded. The only tedious part of the recording process was Tom's constant challenging of all of Mark's ideas. Luckily, when we played the new demo for John, this time he was blown away. He immediately told us that he was picking up our option and signing us to a real recording deal. We were afraid that we'd be stuck making the record with Tom as well as Mark, but fate intervened. Tom had become so bitter about the experience of working with us that he went to John Kalodner behind our backs and told him he didn't stand behind the recordings that we'd turned in. Since John loved them, that was the end of Tom.

It was at this point that we decided to move to LA to record our album. This was also the time that we conceded to letting our original band members go and to making the record with the studio musicians who played on our demo. To be truthful, John had always had it in for our band. He had tried to convince us to get rid of them when we first got our development deal, because he didn't like the way they looked. Then we had refused. Now with a record deal as incentive, John made it clear that we had a huge choice to make. In the end we chose a record deal over loyalty and friendship. But with our band went all of the joy and fun of making music. To this day I still feel bad about firing our friends. We made the wrong decision, chose flash over substance, and I still regret it.

From that point on, my music career felt like all work and no play. All anyone talked about or cared about was the bottom line . . . profits.

Heidi and I moved to Los Angeles in December of 1990 and started working with Mark on writing songs for the album right after New Year's. Heidi and I, along with our roommate, Amy, moved into a small two-bedroom house in Sherman Oaks, not too far from my mom, who was by then living in Malibu.

Mark had an office in West LA with a small demo studio. We would go there several days a week to work on writing song melodies, occasionally being joined by two of the studio musicians we were now working with. We would then spend hours at home working on lyrics for these new songs.

I really missed living in New York, but I knew that the move to LA was good for my career. Everyone we were working with lived in LA. Plus, there was another big bonus about being back on the West Coast: I got to see a lot more of my friends and family, especially Joan, who had been diagnosed with cancer two years before. She was doing very well after initial radiation and oral chemotherapy treatments, and Heidi and I began spending time with her.

After a few months of being in LA, I started to notice some changes in Heidi's overall temperament. She was becoming very irritable and short-tempered, and we seemed to be getting into fights over nothing. I assumed that it must be because of all of the pressure we were under with our record deal, but I turned out to be very wrong. Heidi finally confessed to me that Mark had been inappropriately making sexual advances toward her. She explained that every time I left the room, Mark would flirt and make sexually suggestive statements to her. Mark was sexually harassing my girlfriend.

I was outraged by this news. He knew we were a couple, and I couldn't believe that he could be so inappropriate and disrespectful in light of that fact. I suggested that we immediately go to the record company and tell them what was happening so that we could fire him, but Heidi didn't want to do that. She quickly reminded me how Mark had saved our asses twice—with the first demo he remixed for us and then with the demo that got us our record deal. We became convinced that if it wasn't for our collaboration with Mark, we would have never gotten a recording deal.

Heidi and I continued to go on like this day after day, and I tried not to leave Heidi's side, though bathroom breaks were unfortunately inevitable. We were putting everything that we had into our careers, and we had already sacrificed so much to get where we were. Heidi and I had both given up our sexual identities and were now deeply embedded in the closet. Heidi had forsaken her feminist beliefs and she willingly accepted daily sexual harassment, and we had both given up our integrity when we chose a record deal over our closest friends. The next casualty of our career was the only thing we still had left—our relationship.

I wish I could say that Mark eventually stopped his harassment. This was not the case—he just got worse once he realized we were too dependent on him to say anything to anyone about what he was doing to Heidi. Mark was actually an extreme example of how most of the men in the record industry behaved. As women we were expected to act in a sexual and subservient way toward men. Looking back, I see that this was excruciating and left me feeling dirty, as if I had sold my soul. We clearly had lost our sense of worth and talent. We were convinced that Mark really did have the power to make or break our career, and to get in the way of our dream to become successful recording artists. The wedge between Heidi and me was not caused only by Mark, but his hitting on her was impacting our relationship. The music business was unrelenting; we practiced almost seven days a week. We were still in the closet. And slowly, Heidi and I had less and less to give each other. The very core of our relationship was ebbing away. Instead of pulling us together, as it might have if we had been older and more mature, our romantic connection was eroding.

In the spring of 1991 Heidi and I went on a short trip to San Francisco. I thought of it as a romantic escape, romance between us having been low on the priority list for a long time now. On the drive up, in an almost casual way, Heidi threw out a bomb, saying that once we were really famous and had groupies of our own, she would like more freedom within our relationship.

Was she talking about an open relationship? This declaration jarred me and cut me to the quick; I realized that Heidi didn't look at our relationship in quite the same way I did. This triggered me to detach from her. It wasn't until the early fall that I realized I had completely fallen out of love with her, but that trip was a turning point in our relationship for me.

In May, on the night of Cinco de Mayo, Heidi and I were at home working on a lyric deadline for songs we were about to play for John Kolodner. After we had finished working, our doorbell rang and it was Joan and Scotti. Joan and Scotti were now next-door neighbors, and, in fact, Scotti owned the house in which Joan lived. We had been invited to Joan's get-together that night but had had to work, so at around 11 P.M., with beer and tequila in hand, Joan brought the party to us. After we had been drinking for a while, we all started to realize that we were hungry, so Joan and I went into our kitchen to find something we could make for everyone. As food cooked in the oven, we went to sit in the backyard while we waited. We started to hold hands in a friendly, casual manner, but then something suddenly changed, and I realized that not only was I starting to feel a sense of excitement and arousal, Joan was, too. This was yet another turning point in my relationship with Heidi.

Toward the end of that summer Heidi, Mark, and I delivered to Kalodner basic demos of about twenty songs that we had written. He liked the new music and finally gave us the green light to start recording our record.

Over the next few months, Joan and I had a few more encounters in which we acknowledged not only our attraction to each other but also our feelings. At one point, Joan said to me, "How far do you want to take this? I could take it the whole way."

I knew what she was asking me. She was ready. But I was still with Heidi, not that we'd been intimate in a long time. As much as I wanted to be with Joan and felt enormously attracted to her, I was worried about how breaking up might affect my recording career with Heidi. Once again, I put something else, this time my career, before my own feelings. Also, knowing how important the record was to Heidi, I felt that breaking up and turning truly, fully toward Joan would undermine everything Heidi and I had worked so hard for the past three years to achieve. It was a kind of cruel irony. Heidi and I work so hard to get to where we're finally going to make our album for a major record label— our joint goal for the past several years—and then our relationship starts to crumble.

So I hesitated. I wanted to be with Joan. I was drawn to her deeply. I think I even knew I was falling in love with her. But my attachment to Heidi, in all its complications, held me back.

Heidi began to notice my more frequent absences, my spending more and more time with Joan, and she began to suspect something was going on. And soon enough it was.

One night in November, after months of flirtations with Joan, I finally had the guts to say to Heidi, "I think our relationship has turned into a friendship and a working relationship. We should acknowledge it so we both can move on."

Heidi became very sad and upset, which shocked me. She'd seemed so uninterested for such a long time.

Then she confessed that a month before she'd actually hooked up with someone—not a full-blown affair—but she'd gotten involved with our hairdresser.

Of course I wasn't angry; I had wanted to do the same thing with Joan. To me, this illustrated that not only were we not in love anymore, but we were both ready and wanting to move on. For reasons that I have never really understood, Heidi disagreed. She didn't want to break up; she wanted us to recommit ourselves to our relationship. But for me, it was too late.

I see now that Heidi and I were young and really didn't understand how to take care of our relationship. The intense pressure of working day in and day out and then returning home was fracturing our bond as lovers. Not to mention the situation with Mark and how powerless we both felt because of it. And after her "I want to sleep with groupies" implication, I had begun to withdraw, and was no longer so easygoing in the face of her being so controlling. At this point I should have just been honest about how I was feeling and explained that for me, the romantic part of our relationship was over, but I didn't. Heidi pleaded for me to stick it out with her, drawing on our history together, that we'd finally accomplished our dream of making a record, and that she might not be able to work with me if we were not together.

Instead of standing up for myself, I agreed not to even broach the subject of the breakup until after our record was made. But I did start having an affair with Joan. I felt weak, small, and afraid of everything, and I never wanted to make anyone angry with me. So I took the coward's way out and caused Heidi, Joan, and myself unnecessary prolonged pain. For the most part, Joan understood my hesitancy to go through with the breakup with Heidi while we were still making the record. As with so many other times during this period of my life, I look back at my decision to be dishonest and deceptive and I cringe.

I'd been seeing a therapist since the beginning of the summer, trying to work through my hesitation in being honest with Heidi. So much of the issue for me was a fear of Heidi's anger, her temper, her ability to unleash. This fear kept me somehow fixed and unable to take care of myself, and I was trying to work through that. I think I was afraid that Heidi might do something to intentionally hurt our career, though I now know she never would have. As with my fear of coming out to my mom, some of this fear was irrational. Any kind of conflict made me very uncomfortable, and even the idea that Heidi might be angry with me shut me down.

Joan was kind, compassionate, and understanding. She may have gotten angry at times and showed her frustration at how I was handling Heidi, but she never lost her temper. More important, I was not afraid of her.

We started recording our album in November, and the atmosphere in the studio was not fun, to say the least. There seemed to be tension between everyone—Heidi and me, Heidi and Mark, and Mark and I. I also remember feeling like an outsider in the studio. Mark was completely focused on Heidi, who was completely focused on every aspect of the recording process. The two of them were either as thick as thieves, both getting off on the music, or Mark was refusing to work because Heidi was refuting his advances. Nobody seemed to care much about my opinion or my feelings. Except for when I was recording a track, I started to feel like I was just there to keep Mark from blatantly sexually harassing Heidi.

In total the record took about ten months to make. Despite my promise to wait until we were finished, I started again to try and break up with Heidi. I wanted to be with Joan; I loved her in a way that made my relationship with Heidi seem very much a part of the past. But whenever I tried to break up with Heidi, she responded with an offhand "Not now. Let's finish the record."

Other times, Heidi seemed to hear me a bit more clearly and she'd say, "I don't think I could work with you if we broke up." It was a no-win situation. Boundaries were always hard for me when I was younger, but with Heidi, I was really put to the test. She tried every tactic, and they all worked, plus I had an irrational fear that something bad would happen if I really did leave her. So I stayed.

In the middle of this hell, Joan planned to spend six weeks in Maui, where Scotti had a condo. I stayed on at Joan's house while she was gone, finding it ever harder to be around Heidi. When

Heidi decided to go home to New York, I jumped at the opportunity to visit Joan in Hawaii. Heidi was pissed off that I didn't go home with her to see her parents like I'd always done in the past. By now she was completely convinced that there was something going on between me and Joan, but I continued to lie and tell her she was imagining things. At that time, I really believed that if Heidi knew about Joan and me, she wouldn't be able to finish the record. That said, continuing to lie to her was a horrible thing for me to do, and I understand now that there was no excuse for it. Sometimes when you're too afraid of hurting someone to be honest, you inadvertently end up hurting everyone around you, including yourself.

When I landed in Maui, Joan picked me up at the airport with flowers in her hands. We went back to Scotti's condo, and Joan presented me with gifts, hugs, and passion. No one had ever made me feel as special; I was the center of her attention. It was all about me. This was something I simply was not used to. I enjoyed every moment of that week I spent with Joan in Hawaii, and I got a taste of what my life could be like if I could ever just find the courage to be honest.

We finally finished recording the album at the end of the summer. Our next step was putting together a new band to perform live in advance of our album release in the spring. Things between Heidi and me were at a stalemate, and she was even beginning to date a bit, but I still was unable to be honest with her and end things completely once and for all.

The only solace I had during this time was when I could steal away and spend time with Joan. The more my relationship with

Heidi disintegrated, the more I claimed I needed space, and the more I would go and stay at Joan's house. Joan was kind, nurturing, and loving, and she treated me the way I'd always wanted to be treated—like a man. This was a new experience for me. When I first started dating Heidi, I opened a door for her, which as a feminist, she found offensive, so I never did it again. Joan, on the other hand, loved chivalry and understood that when I opened the door for her, it not only made her feel good, it made me feel good as well.

I didn't quite understand my dynamic with Joan at the time; I probably would have explained it like this: "She treats me like a butch, and she is a femme, and that's part of the reason we work so well together." Obviously, I hadn't yet realized that I was a transgender male. But what I did know was that Joan really responded to my masculine energy in a very feminine way, and this made me feel incredibly at ease, powerful, and sexual with her.

Then we learned that Joan's cancer had returned.

I was at her house in the Valley, and Joan walked in the front door, returning from seeing her doctor after a regular checkup. She sat down and said, "I have bad news. The cancer is back."

Joan was visibly shaken and upset. I couldn't say a word and simply walked over to where she was sitting and put my arms around her, trying to comfort her.

We spent the rest of the day together, trying to be hopeful. I tried to remind Joan that the chemo had worked before and there was no reason it wouldn't work again. Then we made love—over and over, as if we were trying to beat back our fears, her disease, and make everything but our bubble cease to exist.

The reality of Joan's illness cut through my irrational fear of angering Heidi. I finally had the guts to tell her what she'd known all along: that I was in love with Joan and wanted to be with her, and that we, Heidi and I, as a couple, were over.

This period in my life is filled with shame, pain, and the sense that I was utterly powerless. The visual I associate with these years is me as a pinball, ricocheting from one person to another, so small and light that I had no control over my own direction.

In most ways, I felt that I had gotten in over my head, in a relationship to which I had surrendered my own will, and then to make it that much more complicated our producer had set his sights on my woman, making me feel impotent. When I look back at this time in my life, it's still easy for me to feel angry and frustrated with how I behaved. I was so fearful in my early twenties, and that fear led me to do, and tolerate, all sorts of things in a way that I would find impossible today. Here was a man who I had known almost all of my life constantly hitting on my girlfriend, and because I wanted to attain success in the music industry, I was too afraid to stand up for myself. At the time I had no idea the effect that all of this was having on my psyche. Today, finally as the man I've always wanted to be, I feel like taking a swing at someone when I relive these moments. I am not alone in how I negatively remember this time. Heidi, who I am still close with, also has lingering frustration and resentments about everything that happened. If she had testosterone coursing through her veins, I'm sure she'd want to take a swing at Mark, too.

From this distance, I see how affected I was by the damage done to me during childhood: the sense of being helpless and unsafe in a way that left me powerless over the chaos of my circumstances. I absorbed this sense of my own vulnerability to such a degree that it directed most of my behavior and kept me from listening to my own feelings. It has taken me a long time to forgive myself for not being truthful with Heidi; for not standing up for myself and my relationship with Joan, which was one of the most loving, giving aspects of my life. But finally, Joan's illness and the depth of my love for her began to sink in, slowly propping me up, manning me up, so to speak, for the task ahead.

CHAPTER SEVEN

Joan

After we finished putting the band together, Mark started working with us to craft a live show. At the same time, Heidi and I started doing photo shoots and interviews together, in preparation of the record's release. Though I enjoy giving interviews now, back then it was a different story. I didn't mind talking about our record, but many of the questions I was asked were about my parents' involvement in our record or about my sexual orientation. I became so frustrated having to answer over and over again, "What do your parents think about your music? Did they help you get a record deal? What's it like to have Sonny and Cher as parents? Did your mom sing backup on the album?" On and on, over and over. I so desperately wanted to be taken seriously as a songwriter and musician, separate and apart from my parents, and these questions got under my skin immensely. Every person who interviewed us asked if we were a couple, to which by then we could honestly answer "No." When they asked me flat out if I was gay, I came up with something about how I didn't like to label myself.

As unpleasant as doing interviews was, I despised having to do photo shoots even more. Nothing made me feel more uncomfortable and disconnected from myself than having to get into full hair and makeup and whatever outfit the stylist chose for me. Then I'd have to pose like a woman while somebody took my picture. For a man living in a female shell, even a man who didn't yet know he was a man, this ordeal felt degrading and humiliating. I never liked the way I looked in any picture, regardless of how pretty I may have appeared to others; the image staring back at me only reinforced how different my outside was from how I felt on the inside. In fact, until very recently, I never liked any photo of myself, nor was I ever happy with my reflection in the mirror. I may now be older and heavier than I used to be, but when I look in the mirror I really like the way the guy reflecting back at me looks.

Working regular hours for rehearsal and doing press allowed me my nights and weekends off to spend with Joan. The time that I spent with her made me very happy, and we were blissfully in love. We were now officially living together, and everyone in our lives knew about our relationship.

Of course, I was nervous to tell my mom that I was involved with Joan. But one day I drove to Malibu, and, standing in her kitchen, I finally said, "There is something I have to tell you and I don't know if you're going to like it."

My mom became visibly nervous and then said, "Okay?"

When I told her that Joan and I were now together as a couple, my mom laughed and seemed relieved. I actually think she thought it was funny and ironic that her daughter ended up with an old friend of hers.

"Well she's a really nice person and she'll treat you really well," my mom said. "This will be a good life experience for you."

By this time, Joan was back on oral chemotherapy, which had very few side effects. And despite how busy I was getting ready for the launch of our record, she and I did manage a couple weekend getaways to Palm Springs and San Diego. We were happy, compatible, and loved our easygoing life together.

Ceremony, as we now called our band, started playing shows, at first around Southern California, and then on a mini tour that ended with a show at Geffen's annual staff conference in New Orleans. While on this tour, I made two rather alarming discoveries that reinforced what I already suspected: that perhaps I had chosen the wrong profession for myself. First I realized how incredibly lonely I felt on the road. I had gotten into music so I could work with my girlfriend, but now that Heidi and I had broken up, that plan was kind of backfiring on me. I missed Joan and the peace that our life together at home brought to me. I didn't want to spend my nights in lousy motel rooms and my days driving around in a van with my now-ex-girlfriend and a group of guys I barely even knew. I wanted to be home with Joan and our animals.

This realization wasn't all that surprising. I had always been a homebody; but I had also assumed when Heidi and I were together that as long as we were together, any place would feel like home. Second, and even more than this, I was completely shocked to realize how much I hated playing live. I hadn't really noticed this back in New York. When we were playing with our original band, with our closest friends in the audience, we felt like a cohesive unit. Now when I was on stage, all I felt was uncomfortable.

Now, it makes perfect sense that I wouldn't feel at home on

stage—I was pretending to be someone I wasn't. But at the time, this part of who I was didn't occur to me. What did occur to me was that I had been busting my ass for almost five years to be successful in a career that I didn't really enjoy. I realized that I had been trying to live out a dream that wasn't mine, or at least didn't come from a genuine place for me. In spite of this realization, I was no closer to figuring out what my true dream was. I still had no idea who I really was, or what I wanted to do with my life. I felt trapped in the record industry, and with our record release looming, I started to question whether I was more afraid of success than failure.

By the time we completed the tour, Geffen had delayed the release of our record, pushing it back to September. Joan and I decided to do what we did best: go to Hawaii. However, before we were set to go, Joan started to come down with what we thought was the flu. She felt tired, achy, and was running a low-grade fever. She just didn't have the energy for such a big trip, nor did her doctor think it was such a good idea, so we canceled our plans.

After a couple of days, Joan started feeling a little better, and I called my mother and asked her if we could use her house in Aspen. She quickly agreed, and Joan and I drove there, along with our Indian ring-necked parrot, Jude, who made a lot of noise and especially liked eating French fries. The first thing we did together in Aspen was take a relaxing bath in my mother's oversized Jacuzzi tub with a gorgeous view of the mountains. The next day, I took Joan to my favorite fishing spot—a man-made reservoir nestled in the mountains, filled with trout.

But then Joan started to feel symptomatic again. We hoped

that it was the result of the altitude—Aspen is eight thousand feet up. Joan called her doctor, an oncologist and hematologist, who sent her to a local doctor to get some blood work done. Joan's doctor called us the next morning with the results of Joan's blood test, and the news was not good. He explained that her non-Hodgkin lymphoma, which had previously been of a small-celled nonaggressive variety, had morphed into a new aggressive strain of the disease. He wanted Joan home for more tests immediately.

It would take us at least two days to drive from Aspen back to California, so I again turned to my mom for help, and as always in tough times, she was there for me. My mom has always been great when the chips are down, and like the many times when I was a kid running into the house bleeding from a bike accident or from being hit by a baseball smack in the face, my mom became calm and took control in a way that I had come to depend on.

The next day, when Joan and I arrived at the small Aspen airport, we found waiting for us two tickets on the first airplane back to Los Angeles. By the end of the week my car was back in our LA driveway.

A bone marrow biopsy showed that the cancer had now invaded Joan's bones, which explained why her body had been aching so much lately and also why she had been running a low-grade fever. Her doctor wanted to start Joan right away on a course of intravenous chemotherapy, the kind that would make her feel nauseous and weak, and cause her to lose her hair. I felt really scared about Joan starting this treatment, especially since shortly after her first series of chemo I would be leaving for a three-week radio promotion tour to kick off the release of my record and its first single, a song called "Could've Been Love." I was a bit relieved when the doctor assured both of us that this type of treatment put 95 percent of patients with non-Hodgkin lymphoma into remission.

Almost immediately after Joan had the first of these chemotherapy treatments, her symptoms went away and she started to feel much better. As much as I hated to leave her at that time, I did feel better about going on my promotion tour knowing that she was improving.

The tour that Geffen planned for Ceremony was designed to get radio stations to add our single to their playlists, and it was extremely grueling to say the least. We were hitting two to three cities a day, five days a week. Heidi, our guitar player Nick, and I would start each day by performing our single live and being interviewed for a morning drive-time radio show; then we would fly to the next city and have lunch with the programmers of another radio station, perform our single again, and do an interview for that station's afternoon drive-time show; and then we'd fly to another city and have dinner with the people from the radio station we'd be appearing on the next morning. The schedule was exhausting, and many of the radio programmers that we had to wine, dine, and practically beg to add our single to their play rosters were quite unsavory characters. They'd give us shit about my family, come on to Heidi and me, and just plain treat us like pieces of meat. As was always the case when I was working, I had to don my costume and makeup and play the part of a female wannabe rock star. Though I could play my role pretty convincingly, the pretense and schmoozing wore on me quickly.

Before it was time for Joan's next chemotherapy treatment, her symptoms began to come back. This started a pattern where she'd have her chemo, start to feel better, and then feel sick again a few weeks later. Then she'd go through chemo again. The frightening part was that the cycles of responding well to the chemo got shorter and shorter. It became clear to me, though not yet to her doctors, that Joan's treatments weren't working, and I was anxious to get home and talk to the doctors about trying something new. I was also very disappointed to find out that after we had traveled to more than thirty different radio stations, not one of those stations added our single to their playlist.

By the time I got home, I was starting to feel pretty run down, and I quickly got sick myself. I went to three different doctors before I was properly diagnosed as having mononucleosis. I was so exhausted from the grueling nature of the tour and my nonstop worrying about Joan that my body just finally broke down. I was too sick to care for Joan and she was too sick to take care of me.

Once again, my mom was there for me, telling me to come home to her house in Malibu and to bring Joan with me. She set us up in a comfortable bedroom and took care of us until I felt strong enough to go back home and resume taking care of Joan.

Before I had completely recovered from my mono, Geffen sent us to New York to do a few good TV spots, performing and doing interviews on Regis and Kathie Lee, the *Today* show, and *Good Morning America*. These performances were really difficult for me because my mono got worse with the traveling. Before returning home, Geffen had us perform at a string of huge radio-sponsored shows in random locations around the country.

Unfortunately, most of the other performers we were scheduled with were dance or pop acts who were singing to fully produced tracks. When Heidi and I got on stage with our acoustic guitars, we'd bring the energy of the whole event to a screeching halt. Time after time, we'd get up on stage, with the crowd expecting dance music, and there we'd be—bringing the crowd down. It was painful—we were a mismatch and clearly not finding our audience.

Joan's doctor soon did another bone marrow biopsy and found that after several rounds of treatment, the cancer was still present. He explained to us that, at this point, Joan's best chance at beating the cancer was to undergo a stem cell transplant. However, in order to do the transplant, he had to first get her into remission, because stem cells are made in one's bone marrow and right now Joan's was riddled with cancer. So the new plan was to start Joan on a different type of chemotherapy and hope that it put her into remission so she could have a stem cell transplant around Christmas.

But right before Joan was about to begin this new phase, she became so sick and was in so much pain that she had to be hospitalized. Her doctor was out of town, so one of the other doctors in his practice came to Joan's room at Cedars-Sinai Hospital to see her. He reiterated much of what we had been told by Joan's doctor, with one stark difference. This new doctor explained, unabashedly void of any sensitivity at all, that they were going to try one more round of chemo, and if that didn't work, there was nothing more to do. Joan was so sick at that point that I don't think she truly understood what he was saying, but I definitely did.

The truth rocked me: if this chemo didn't work, they would simply let Joan die. No more push for remission. No stem cell transplant. Death. I had to leave the hospital before I broke down in front of Joan, and I went to see Heidi, who by now had become a trusted friend and business partner. This was the first time I talked aloud about the possibility that Joan might die.

The new chemotherapy obliterated the cancer cells in Joan's bone marrow; however it also made her so sick that she ended up in intensive care for a couple days. During this time, Geffen decided to send our band off to Flint, Michigan, to play at a local radio station's Halloween show. The last thing any of us wanted to do was play another radio station–sponsored show where we'd certainly be the only band doing an acoustic set. I was especially upset, terrified to leave Joan's side.

Yet off to Flint I went. We were completely dejected when we saw the dreadful motel that had been booked for us. Our disappointment continued to grow after we had a horrible sound check, and found out that the headlining act was the Village People, whose music and stage performance couldn't have been more different from ours.

But when we finally took the stage, something truly amazing happened. As our guitarist Nick started playing the opening riff to "Could've Been Love," the audience started screaming and going crazy; the three of us literally turned around to see who had come on stage behind us, to find no one there. Then, once I started singing, I noticed that people in the audience were actually singing along with me. None of us had any idea what was going on, but it was amazing to play for an audience of a couple thousand people who knew and loved our music.

When we got off the stage, we asked somebody from the radio station what had just happened and how these people knew our song. We found out that we had a hit single in Flint, Michigan. I can't say that our performance in Flint made everything I had gone through as a musician worth it. However, I have always been grateful that I got that little taste of what it must be like to be a rock star. It's an amazing feeling to have thousands of people singing along with you to a song that you wrote, and I will never forget it.

Joan was in and out of the hospital throughout the fall. The chemotherapy was working, though it was taking a huge toll on her general health. She was now extremely thin and frail. When Joan was in the hospital, I stayed with her every night, sleeping on a cot in her room. If she was sent home for a few days or weeks, then I undertook her complete care on my own. Our house was starting to resemble a hospital, with medical gear and medication everywhere, and me acting like a nurse, administering oral, IV, and injectable medications throughout the day—everything to keep her alive.

Not terribly aware of what I was doing, I soon started to dip into some of Joan's Percodan in order to ease the anxiety and pain of watching my girlfriend die in front of me. This action soon began to alter the course of my life.

When Joan was in the hospital, I didn't have to stay every night, but I didn't have the sense to go home or to my mom's or a friend's to have a night off. I just didn't know how to take care of myself. I believed that I could keep Joan alive with all my care and love, and I was convinced there was no one else but me to do it. Of course, I'd probably do the same thing today. But I was so bad at self-care, at tending to my own physical and emotional needs, that I was unwittingly setting the stage for some even worse times ahead.

By early December, Joan had gone into remission, and doctors started to harvest her stem cells for the transplant. Joan checked in to the hospital a couple of days before Christmas to start her stem cell transplant, and the first thing they did was bombard her body with a deadly dose of chemotherapy in order to obliterate her immune system. The process of the transplant is that after this immune attack, your stem cells are put back into your body so that they can create a new healthy, cancer-free immune system. Joan became deathly ill from this process, and she was at such a high risk for infection that we couldn't even have flowers or fresh fruits or vegetables in her hospital room.

Christmas and New Year's passed dismally, and then on January 17, 1994, everyone in Los Angeles and the surrounding areas was awoken by a 6.7 earthquake, emanating from Northridge. I was still at Cedars sleeping on my cot in Joan's room when the earthquake hit, and I was literally thrown out of bed. It was the biggest earthquake I had ever experienced, and while it was happening I was sure that the building would collapse and crush us all.

Following the quake, and after five weeks in the hospital, Joan was stable enough to come home.

Meanwhile, Geffen Records informed us that they had stopped working to promote our first single and would release a new one shortly. Then our manager decided he no longer wanted to work with us. In spite of this bad news, Heidi and I were determined not to let our record die. Thinking that Joan was stable enough for me to leave for a few days, Heidi and I decided to go on a brief tour to the Bay Area to play some gigs to support the record.

If I were to be brutally honest with myself, I'd say I was relieved to get away. I had not slept through the night in months. The isolation and stress of caring for Joan was depleting me. I was looking forward to getting away and getting back into music. I ended up having a lot of fun on that tour with Heidi and the guys in our band. It was a relief to cut loose for a bit and act like the twenty-four-year-old that I was, playing rock 'n' roll music and drinking with my friends. And it was a relief to be friends with Heidi after our history together.

When I got back, Joan looked horrible. It was the first time that she seemed really disoriented and mentally not quite present or clear. She was now sleeping all the time. The doctors had told us she would be weak for a long time after the stem cell transplant, so I was not surprised by her need for sleep. But her mental disorientation really bothered me.

One morning we woke and her disorientation seemed particularly acute. She didn't know if it was day or night and thought people were riding motorcycles in her yard. We were set to go to the doctor the next morning, but I called to tell him about Joan's delirium. He suggested that maybe the cancer had spread to her brain.

He told me to hold tight and that he'd see her in the morning. Then I left to go give blood for Joan at the hospital. Her red and white blood cell counts where still very low from the transplant, and she needed regular blood transfusions.

Returning home, as I approached our house, I saw there was an ambulance in the driveway. Scotti was taking care of Joan while I was gone. She explained that Joan had fallen down and was having a lot of difficulty breathing so she called 911. The EMT docs were about to take Joan to a small hospital in the Valley, near our house. By the time the ambulance arrived at the hospital, Joan's doctor had overridden the orders and told the EMTs to take Joan to Cedars-Sinai in West Hollywood.

Joan was admitted into the ICU. That night, Joan and I had our last lucid conversation. Over the next couple of days Joan slipped further into delirium, until she was virtually unconscious. She died February 4, 1994. I was one month shy of my twenty-fifth birthday. Joan's autopsy revealed that she died cancer-free, from pneumonia, which she had contracted as a result of the stem cell transplant.

CHAPTER EIGHT

Falling Apart

Not too long after Joan's funeral, I'd moved into a small apartment in West Hollywood after a brief stay with Heidi. I immediately began pursuing a new relationship. This says a lot about my state of mind at the time. Terrified of being alone, I became obsessed with Tracy, a woman I'd met through mutual friends. I had actually met Tracy a few years before, but I was reintroduced to her through a friend and found her attractive. I began pursuing her despite there being a host of red flags, not the least of which was her telling me that she was an alcoholic and still in love with her ex.

I see now that, obviously, running headfirst into a new relationship was my way of trying to avoid the tremendous amount of pain I was in over losing Joan.

My career was at a complete standstill. The week Joan died, Geffen formally dropped our band from the label. Any marketing of our record had come to an abrupt halt, and I didn't have the strength or willingness to start all over again. Plain and simple, I had no idea what I wanted to do now, or how to reinvent myself. I did know, however, that I was done with music. Since I had no idea how to move forward in my life, I went to bartending school and got a job at Girl Bar, a popular lesbian club in LA at the time. I wanted to make some money, but this was a total disaster for me. I was the world's worst bartender since I'm horrible under any kind of fast-paced pressure, but more than that, I was constantly being singled out by women because of who I was. I hated this kind of attention, and soon quit. Then a friend got me a job working in a corporate real estate office, doing office work for ten dollars an hour. This was quite possibly the most boring and uninspiring job on the planet, but again I took the job because I needed to make money and to get out of the house and do something.

Not helping my general depression and rudderless life was the fact that Tracy was a big partier, and, still trying to avoid the pain of Joan's death, I began to party with her.

During this year, my endometriosis also started to get really bad. Every month when my period came, I experienced intense pain. My doctor started prescribing Vicodin for me.

Around this time, Judy Weider, then editor of the *Advocate*, had been courting me to come out in the magazine. We had gotten together a few times and talked about doing an interview for the publication, but I didn't feel ready. Though I was no longer actively trying to hide my sexual orientation, I didn't feel like I had anything going on in my life to talk about, and my confidence was at a low point. I think, too, that I was responding to advice my mom had given me. She had always instilled in me a philosophy that you should never do press if you don't have something important to talk about or a specific project to promote. Over the years, when the press has approached me to do a story—either in print or other media—I've often turned to my mom for her feedback—she has reliable radar for when a story is worth it and when it seems like it might be more of a fluff piece. Though many today don't subscribe to this idea about speaking to the media, I still think in most cases it's really good advice.

But Judy's interest in me and what I could do for the GLBT community seemed sincere, so after a year of bumping around from one job to another with no direction, I approached Judy about a job at the *Advocate*. I told her I'd do anything—fetch coffee, stuff envelopes—I didn't care what it was as long as I had a place to go and make a contribution. I had spent so many years back in the closet, that the idea of doing work that would serve the community now had become very appealing to me.

Then in January 1995, a musician named Melissa Ferrick had a new record coming out, and Judy Weider asked me if I wanted to interview her. I did, and this opportunity ultimately led to me becoming a writer for the magazine. I had been interviewed so much in my life that I took to that part of the job easily. I did, however, have a lot to learn about writing and magazine publishing. After a few months, I was finally feeling like my work had value and that I had something to say. So that February, I came out on the cover of the *Advocate*, telling my story to the world. I was soon being contacted by all sorts of gay and lesbian organizations who wanted me to get involved in their cause. My first real taste of gay activism was when the Human Rights Campaign (HRC) asked me to go to Washington, DC, to take part in a press conference for the reintroduction of the Employment Non-Discrimination Act to Congress. Then I started working independently, doing speaking engagements at GLBT events and conferences. A year later, in 1996, HRC hired me to be its

National Coming Out spokesperson, as well as to help motivate gay and lesbian people to reelect President Bill Clinton.

My political activism career happened very quickly, but I took to my new role very naturally. I was probably a bit of a political zealot (something my mom pointed out to me at one time). But I think I was truly astonished by how often gay and lesbian people were treated as less than equal, not only in their lack of civil rights but also in the portrayal of gays and lesbians in the media. I felt very passionately about speaking out for equal rights. Neither of my parents ever told me directly that they were proud of me for this big career change, though my dad seemed to get a kick out of me suddenly becoming so politically active.

The more my career took the shape of activism, the more my spirits began to lift and the better I felt about myself. My work life began to gain traction, and I felt I was carving out a place for myself in that world, one that had growing meaning for me— not the least reason for which was how it had nothing to do with the music business or my parents. At the time, this was very important to me. After my experience in the record industry, when I was constantly being compared to my parents and their music, I really wanted something that was mine. I was young— twenty-six years old—and I felt a growing confidence that I could actually help people, make a contribution to the GLBT community, and become part of something larger than myself. When I got my first book deal, to write *Family Outing*, this sense of working for a larger purpose was cemented. That book was not only about my own coming out story, but it was also a guide to help other people who were struggling with coming out, especially to their parents.

Around this time, Tracy and I moved to San Francisco on a whim. We had been to the Dinah Shore lesbian golf event in Palm Springs and met a group of interesting lesbians who were from the Bay Area. Tracy and I felt that given my new political profile San Francisco might make a better fit. I had never really settled into LA since I'd moved back with Heidi for our record, and I think I was still missing the edge of New York. So moving to Northern California seemed like a good idea at the time. Also, since my relationship with Tracy had always been somewhat tenuous, we thought somehow a move would bring us closer together; of course moves for impetuous reasons never solve problems. Our problems simply followed us.

Very quickly after unpacking, I knew the move was a mistake. San Francisco was socially and politically just too radical for me. I realized that though I had always considered myself to be a left-wing liberal, by San Francisco standards I was more of a moderate. I also think that my own political position at the time was influenced by the Human Rights Campaign, the organization I was working for, which is pretty conservative in terms of gay politics. I also really missed Los Angeles, and my friends and family there. I didn't realize that LA had become home to me again until I left.

In any case, I felt like a fish out of water the whole time I was living in San Francisco. Tracy had a normal day job, so I was left alone in our apartment for long stretches of time. I soon began to feel isolated and really depressed. When the Gay and Lesbian Alliance Against Defamation (GLAAD) offered me a great position with a big salary at the end of that year, I didn't hesitate to accept. All I had to do was convince Tracy to move back to Los Angeles, which I did pronto.

On the surface, all seemed better. But soon I began to realize that even though my career was thriving, I was not. All my life I had virtually ignored my feelings and soldiered on. But something inside of me was beginning to shift. The enormous pain of losing Joan had never gone away, and I began to increase my drug use, not only using the Vicodin for the week I had my period but at other times as well. I started to use Vicodin regularly, becoming dependent on its high and its numbing effect on my overall discomfort. The pills first blocked my physical pain. Then began doing more.

On January 5, 1998, the very day I turned in the manuscript for *Family Outing*, my father died in a freak skiing accident. I got the call from my stepmother, Mary, right after I had gone to bed. When Mary told me that my father was dead, I went totally and completely numb, and then did what I always did: I focused on other people around me.

I put all my energy into how Mary and my brother and sister Chesare and Chianna were coping. After making plans to meet them in Palm Springs the next day, I hung up the phone and started to track my mom down to tell her. She was in Europe at the time, and I had to call my aunt Gee to get a number for her. When I told Gee what had happened, she asked me if I wanted her to break the news to my mom, because she thought my mom would be extraordinarily upset. Thinking she must be exaggerating, I called my mom myself to tell her what had happened. I have never heard my mom as devastated by anything before or since as she was by the news of my father's death. After trying to comfort my sobbing mom as best as I could, I finally told her that I would have Gee call her back.

I left for Palm Springs the next morning. Heidi, her new girlfriend Caitlin, and Karen, a girl I had just started dating, accompanied me to my dad's compound. Tracy and I had finally broken up about two months before my father died. My mom and my brother Elijah, along with my dad's oldest child (from his first marriage), Christie Bono, and my dad's closest friends, Vinnie, Donnie, Dennis, and Charlotte, all made it there by that night. We all stayed in Palm Springs for the next week, getting through a private and then very public funeral together.

The reality of my father's death really didn't hit me until I was sitting in the small church during the private service that we had for him. I was overcome with grief. Because of political differences that had arisen between us as my dad took on his role as congressman and I took on mine as gay activist, he and I hadn't spoken for over a year.

When I had started working at the *Advocate*, my dad suggested that I interview him, so I did. But when we met at a restaurant in Washington, DC, so I could conduct the interview for the magazine, he seemed totally unprepared. I was asking him his political and personal stances on all issues that impacted gays and lesbians, one of which was gay marriage. He basically said that he didn't have a problem with gay marriage as long as any new legislation wouldn't cost taxpayers more money. He was being straightforward and practical. But he soon got in very hot water from his religious-right constituents (something I learned later from openly gay congressman Barney Frank from Massachusetts), and by 1996, he had cosponsored the Defense of

Marriage Act (DOMA), which, needless to say, felt like a betrayal of me. DOMA was the Republicans' effort to ban marriage for gays and lesbians by federally defining marriage as being lawful only between a man and a woman. I was hurt and angry. After he spoke out so blatantly in favor of anti-gay legislation, I started doing press to basically blow the whistle on him, saying that he had reversed his position.

Unfortunately, he and I never talked about the situation; in fact, when he died, a year had passed without either one of us saying a word to the other directly.

As I listened to family members and close friends go up to talk about my father, I began to realize how stupid we had both been letting politics affect our relationship. My dad and I had always been so close and had such an honest relationship. I was devastated that we hadn't had a chance to talk through our differences before he died. As the reality of his being gone started to sink in, I cried for the first time since the moment I found out about his death.

That was a week that I'll never forget. Though it was sad for everyone, I found a lot of peace in being together with the family and friends that I had known my entire life, many of whom I hadn't seen for years. My mom was there of course—and she, too, needed the comfort of being surrounded by everyone who knew and loved my dad, laughing and crying all together as we started to tell stories about him. For the next couple of years, every few months, my mom invited the whole group to spend the weekend at her house on Point Dume in Malibu. She bought us a bunch of board games, and we all hung out, staying up late cooking and playing games. It brought us enormous catharsis and really helped us begin to recover from the shock of my dad's death.

I started having chronic headaches after my father's death. One of the consequences of stuffing down your feelings is that they tend to manifest physically, a phenomenon I am now all too familiar with.

When I went to see a neurologist for my chronic pain, I was prescribed more drugs. Heidi and Karen were getting concerned about my drug use (Heidi was sober by this time), but neither of them was aware of the degree of my growing dependence on these drugs in a daily, habitual way. Heidi told my mother that I was taking a lot of drugs for pain (headaches, endometriosis), but when my mother confronted me, I denied the problem, instead describing all my very real physical symptoms. My mom called her doctor, and together they tried to come up with an alternative way to treat me. I was not hopeful.

To make matters worse, during the summer I was fired from GLAAD. The previous season both Ellen DeGeneres and her character on her sitcom had come out publicly. Through my job at GLAAD, I got to spend a lot of time on the set of Ellen's show. It was a treat to be part of such groundbreaking television and I loved having the opportunity to get to know Ellen a bit. I was even on one episode, which earned me my Screen Actors Guild card. But now that the show was in its second season, and the show's ratings were beginning to slip. I was doing an interview with the *San Jose Mercury News* about a letter-writing campaign GLAAD had launched to try to save the show when the journalist asked me point-blank if I thought the network was homophobic and if that was why they were considering dropping the show.

I remember our conversation vividly. It was a Friday afternoon and I was home. I remember acknowledging that the ratings were declining; that *The Drew Carey Show* was probably not the best lead-in; that the network wasn't doing a lot of advertising; and that perhaps the content of the show had become a bit too gay-specific for a national TV audience.

The next thing I knew, my comments were excised from their context and repeated on the cover of *Variety*: "Bono thinks Ellen is too gay!" Everyone in the gay community went berserk. I started getting hate mail, and was criticized by the media. As soon as the GLAAD Media Awards were over, an event I had helped arrange and plan, and where my mother received a big award, I was fired. I felt angry, frustrated, and betrayed by the gay community. No one seemed inclined to explain my comments and clarify how they were taken out of context; and I couldn't believe that all the good I'd achieved for the organization and the community at large could be negated by a misquote. I was devastated. I went on *Larry King Live* to explain what had happened, but to no avail. The new executive director, who I had been suspecting of wanting to fire me, had done just that.

I didn't know what I was going to do—so much of my identity had become wrapped up in being GLAAD's entertainment media director, and now I was being treated like a pariah.

A couple of years later, I was able to put this experience into perspective for myself and see it as part of my learning curve on how to deal with the media. Clearly, the media's opinions of public figures can turn on a dime. By the next year, much of the gay and lesbian media had actually begun to echo my view of the *Ellen* show, saying that it had become "too gay" for a mainstream television audience. The *Advocate* even did a cover story on me with the title "Renegade Activist," and a lot of the article recounted the whole *Ellen* story. About two years later, Ellen and I got the chance to talk, and we worked out any misunderstandings.

Now I realize that for all that was positive about my career as a political activist, I was simply looking to work to fill a void of pain inside of me. I now think of it as a black hole of pain at the center of my being. I stuffed painkillers into that void, as well as my work, but no matter how much I kept feeding the hole, it just kept getting bigger. My work became just like the drugs, and I kept waiting for my professional accomplishments to somehow make me feel better about myself. I became very focused on the next thing, then the next thing, thinking that every goal I chased would finally heal my pain. The worst part of this was that while I was working on a project, I never felt anything at all, because my mind was already on the next one that I hoped would nourish my spirit.

By the following summer of 1999, I was using so much Vicodin that I went into liver failure. I was living in New York that summer, involved in what I thought at the time was a cool tech start-up. I didn't realize that the acetaminophen in the Vicodin could be so damaging. Doubled over in pain, I took myself to the emergency room, where they admitted me. Thank god the liver is an organ that, given half a chance, can regenerate.

As soon as I was released, I switched to a new pain management program: Vicuprofen, which contained ibuprofen instead of acetaminophen.

By Christmas, I was back in the hospital, this time with an ulcer. I'd been taking so much pain medication that it was now actually adding to my pain. I have a vague memory of the doctor telling me at the time that I was using way too many drugs, but I was in no frame of mind to listen to him or his advice.

After I was released for the ulcer, Karen and I went up to Malibu, to my mother's house. It was New Year's Eve and the turn of a new century. I was still riddled with pain and sleeping around the clock. I had asked Karen to wake me up to watch the ball drop. All I remember from the millennium celebration is the ball dropping, then me running to the bathroom to be sick, crawling back into bed, and promptly passing out.

By this time, I was so depressed that I was thinking of checking myself into a mental hospital. It never occurred to me that the problem with my life was that I had become a drug addict. To me the problem *was* life, which was full of pain and death, and I thought that the only thing that was getting me through the darkness was the painkillers.

Then, in the beginning of January, right before I was about to commit myself, Heidi came over to have a talk with me. She very gently said to me that she thought the reason that I was so miserable was because of my drug use. I remember thinking how crazy the idea was—after all, I was convinced that the pills were the only thing that was keeping me from taking my own life. She then made me a promise: she told me that she could guarantee that if I stopped taking drugs and got into a recovery program, I would feel better. I heard very real concern in her voice, and I believed her.

I was also so desperate I would have done anything to feel better.

PART TWO

Starting Over

CHAPTER NINE

The First Step

January 20, 2000, was my first sobriety date. But sometimes getting clean and sober isn't quite so easy, or so linear.

By this point, Karen and I had broken up. And in my typical fashion, I met someone new right away, this time at a recovery support group meeting.

At first, Kathy and I seemed like a good match. Kathy was pretty androgynous-looking, and I wasn't drawn to her physically as I had been to Joan, or even Karen. But I was really impressed by the fact that she had become sober at such a young age (when she was twenty) and was now twelve years sober. I so needed a role model in sobriety, and Kathy easily fit that bill for me. She had told me that she was very involved in support groups and had a big social circle. I was smitten, and so didn't waste much time and asked her to move into my house.

Kathy was quite charismatic and very social, which made me a lot more social, too. We went to a lot of parties and barbecues and started hanging out with a lot of other sober lesbians. In one way, I felt like I was coming out of my drug haze, which had been so isolating. I was trying my best to be outgoing, thinking that if I connected more with people, I'd feel more at ease with myself and less depressed. I wanted to be part of a community of like-minded people. And I thought that's what I'd found.

At one particular barbecue, Kathy and I were hanging out with a bunch of her friends. Everyone was talking, chatting, eating—having a good time, but I remember feeling a bit set apart, like I didn't quite belong. It was always my habit to do more observing than participating, but as I looked around and took inventory, watching the women interact and listening to their lesbian-oriented conversations, a question began to form in my mind: do I have anything at all in common with these women?

I began to realize that no matter what these women looked like, whether they identified as more feminine, butch, or as something in between, they all identified as women. And they all were comfortable with their female identities and even seemed to enjoy being women. I had always assumed that there was a small portion of the lesbian community, some of the butch lesbians like me, who felt as I always had, wishing that I had been born a man. Earlier in my life, when I was with Joan, I had assumed that the butch-dyke women in Joan's circle—Dori and Suzanne, for instance—felt just like I did.

I didn't immediately associate this discomfort with being transgender. In my mind, being transgender required feeling and being much more desperate. Hadn't I been coping just fine as a butch lesbian? I then believed that transitioning meant automatic, inevitable ostracism, and who in their right mind would want to risk that? I may have thought I had something in common with people who were trans, but I did not include myself in that category. Yes, I had never been comfortable in my female body. I didn't like my breasts, and my period caused me only pain. But I had just tried to make the best of it.

Now, as a part of a large and diverse group of lesbians around my own age, I was coming to the conclusion that these women did not feel the same way about their bodies or their identities. And I was actually surprised. This was the first time that I began to question if I might be something other than a lesbian. Of course, by now I knew that transgender people existed and had even known a transgender man who was friends with Joan. But for some reason the idea that *I* might be transgender hadn't begun to register until this very moment.

The previous year, the film *Boys Don't Cry* had come out. I don't think the timing of my realization that I might be transgender was a coincidence: I believe that the film reflected our culture beginning to wrap its head around being transgender as a concept and a reality. I also think that the film was part of what enabled me to think that transitioning was a possibility.

When I was younger, I really knew nothing about transgender or transsexual people or transitioning. In my twenties, I think I just wanted to fit in so badly that I never really allowed myself to feel how uncomfortable I was with my gender identity. But in 2000, a year after Hilary Swank rocked the world with her portrayal of young pre-medical-transition FTM, I finally had enough clarity to realize that there was something different about me and it had nothing to do with my sexual orientation. It was a lot more complicated.

Over the next few weeks and months, I began to play with the possibility that I might be transgender. I'd casually voice questions and comments to my then girlfriend, Kathy. "Maybe I'm transgender." Or "Do you think I might be transgender?"

At first, Kathy seemed nonplussed. I'd say to Kathy, "Maybe I'm transgender, because I've never felt like a girl."

And she was cool about it, simply responding with "Yeah, maybe you are."

At the time, Kathy was working at the Los Angeles Gay & Lesbian Center, in their residential youth facility. She came home one day talking about a guy named Masen Davis, a transgender activist, who had come to the Center to speak. She suggested that maybe I should talk to Masen, so I called him up and said I was doing research for a book and wanted to a understand more about being transgender. I was lying of course.

Masen and I made plans to meet at my house while Kathy was at work. As we talked, I remember being blown away by how many feelings and experiences we shared. Masen described how even as a child he had felt like a boy, as I did. He then described how he had also assumed as he got older that he must be a lesbian, yet he never felt like he really fit in with lesbians. He also experienced the same animosity toward his body as I had; like me, he had gone through a breast reduction, hoping it would ease some of the dysphoria he had always felt toward that aspect of his body. After talking with Masen for a while, I became comfortable enough to come clean. I told him that I thought I might be transgender, too.

Kathy came home in the middle of our meeting, and Masen stayed for an hour or so after she arrived. When she saw how excited I was about my talk with him, and how much we seemed to have in common, Kathy began to look visibly uncomfortable.

From that point on, Kathy was incredibly hostile about the

subject, and slowly, this ate away at our relationship and at me. We started to argue all the time, most of our fights ending with Kathy proclaiming, "Well, I'm not the one who wants a penis." She started to say this so often, it became like a catchphrase— I'm surprised she didn't have it embroidered on a pillow. It was pretty clear to me that when the idea of my being transgender was an abstract notion, Kathy could handle it. But as soon as it was more of a reality—and I actually was considering starting the process—she freaked out.

I then started seeing a transgender therapist named Davis talk about my thoughts around being transgender. It was helpful to talk to someone else about my feelings, especially a transgender man who could share his own experience on the topic, as Davis was. I slowly started to gain more clarity about the fact that I was indeed a transgender person. However, I didn't feel like I was getting any closer to knowing what I should or shouldn't do about it.

The following journal excerpt is a testament to how I was trying to catalogue my fears, in hope, I guess, that they would dissipate. Here's a sample of some of my writing from this time:

Fears

- Losing Kathy
- Having my mom disown me
- Having my mom be totally unsupportive and not understanding why I want to become a man
- The press making my mom miserable
- My family not being supportive or understanding

- My family not wanting me in their lives
- Gee not being supportive or understanding
- My family not believing that I'm really transgender
- Becoming a big joke
- Being thought of as a freak by people who know me and the public at large
- Being followed by the press wherever I go
- Suffering a hate crime
- Not being taken seriously as an activist
- The gay and lesbian community hating me and looking at me as a traitor and having my colleagues turn their backs on me
- Never being able to be seen as anything other than a transgender
- Not being able to work or make a living
- My animals not knowing me
- Not being able to be a good trans activist
- Losing all my credibility
- People being afraid of me
- Losing friends and acquaintances
- Being repulsive to Kathy
- Kathy leaving me for a woman
- Being alone for the rest of my life
- Not being handsome
- Not being able to make my body look the way I want it to look
- Not being able to pass as a man
- Relapsing

That's the actual list. My fears ranged from basic fears about passing as a man to irrational fears about my mother and family turning against me. Needless to say, this myriad of fears was significant, and I could not navigate through them easily at that time.

I began reading everything I could find about transgender people and transitioning. I ended up buying Loren Cameron's book *Body Alchemy* twice because Kathy threw away my first copy.

Throughout all of this, I was still suffering enormous pain during my periods. When I first started getting sober, my therapist at the time suggested I go to a pain management specialist who was supposedly skilled at treating chronic pain for people with addiction issues. This pain doctor put me on a fairly low dose of Oxycontin for the week of my period. At that time I had no idea what Oxycontin was or how potentially addictive it could be, and for over a year I took the drug for the week of my period.

I was still going to meetings and thought of myself as sober.

At home, I was trying to deal with Kathy's growing hostility; we tried couples therapy; she even went to a support group in San Francisco for partners of trans people that a trans friend of hers had told her about.

Despite this, Kathy would always resort to telling me there was something wrong with me, and part of me agreed with her. I'd take her negative feedback and use it to try and suppress my belief that I was transgender.

But slowly, as always happened to me, the emotional pain and stress I was feeling started to manifest itself physically. Right about this time, my pain-management doctor moved, and the partner who took over his practice was not nearly as cognizant of my history with drugs or my overall sensitivity to them. I heard that this doctor ended up losing his license because he was so irresponsible. Of course, I don't blame either doctor for my drug use, but any patient with an addictive history should not be given Oxycontin to treat chronic pain.

I began a familiar cycle: my endometriosis would grow back; the pain would increase; I'd use medicine to manage the pain; and then finally I'd have to have surgery. At this time, when they went in to examine my uterus, they found a cyst on one of my ovaries that needed to be removed. This cycle was repeated a few times during my twenties and thirties.

The new doctor started giving me more pain medicine to deal with the cycle.

And yet I still didn't think I was having a relapse. I was really in pain and working with a doctor. I thought I was safe.

Then, in late 2001, it was decided that I had to have another laparoscopic surgery to clean out more endometriosis. After this procedure, my pain decreased for a while and I started to wean myself off the pain medicines—down from twelve 80-mg Oxycontin pills per day to nine per day. But even though the pain was now less, I couldn't seem to wean off medication altogether, because I liked the way I was feeling when I took it. I wasn't in as much pain, but I was enjoying the drugs. I was hooked again. This should not surprise anyone who understands the disease of addiction; if you keep giving an addict drugs they will become addicted to them.

In 2002, my second book, *The End of Innocence*, was published. Apparently my drug use was starting to become obvious on the book tour, and truthfully, I don't remember much of it at all. When I read the book now, it's apparent to me that I wasn't completely present when I was writing it. The drugs had begun to dominate my life.

Kathy and I eventually broke up. It was a very mutual breakup, and she kept living with me as a roommate instead of a girlfriend. By the time Kathy did move out, she had told my mother that I was now taking Oxycontin for my periods and that I believed I was transgender. Needless to say my mother began to worry about me anew. She sent me to her doctor, who recommended me to a new therapist, Sari (the therapist I've been seeing ever since).

I didn't really want to go to this doctor, but I agreed to appease my mother and keep using my drugs. I was doing the same thing with my sponsor Jane, whom I had only joined up with to get Kathy off my back. I was up to all the drug addict tricks.

Some part of me realized that I was in even worse shape than before my first attempt to get sober. I was now completely physically addicted. I couldn't miss a dose or I would have withdrawal symptoms. I didn't leave my house, and I stopped having a menstrual cycle. I was almost completely alone. I had slowly let most of the people in my life drift away as I started using more and more drugs. By that time even Heidi, who had become like a sister to me after our breakup, was out of my life. I wasn't socializing anymore—I didn't see any of my friends from sober support groups. I only saw people I had to see.

But I was wily enough to keep up the charade, so I continued to meet Jane once a week for dinner and an alcoholic support group meeting. I did this not because I wanted to get sober, but because I wanted to keep on using. I was the kind of practicing drug addict that could only use drugs if nobody else knew about it. If I had quit going to meetings, Jane would have known I had relapsed, and then the jig would be up. So I just kept pretending that I was sober. It was a horrible hypocrisy, and I felt guilty and disappointed in myself all the time.

My mom started to figure out that something very serious was going on. Around this time she offered to pitch in for me to buy a nicer house. I'd bought my first house with the money I made from *Family Outing*, and it had appreciated considerably. My mom suggested I sell it, and that she would kick in some extra money so I could trade up.

But when we'd go and look at houses together, my mom noticed my behavior and started suspecting that I was back on drugs. I don't know exactly what made her suspicious. She probably saw that I had no range of emotion and was monotone and lethargic. I wasn't nodding out in front of my mom, but my color was gray and sallow. My eyes probably also gave me away. When we found a house that we both liked, she gave me an ultimatum that she wouldn't help me buy the house unless I went away to treatment. I didn't take kindly to her ultimatum and told her I'd be happy to stay where I was. At that point there was no way I was going in for residential drug treatment.

Three years had passed since my first sobriety date. At this point, in the beginning of 2003, Thursdays were the only day I got out of my house. Thursday was the day I'd go see Sari, and tell her that I was trying to cut back on my drug use. Then I'd go to dinner and a recovery meeting with Jane, where I'd pretend to be committed to sobriety.

Then I'd go home and collapse. I wasn't bathing except on Thursdays. I hardly saw anyone but Jane and Sari. All day long I watched TV and played video games or read. I was also smoking two to three packs of cigarettes a day at this time. My mattress, sheets, blankets, and carpet had cigarette burns on them.

My diet changed, too. All I felt like eating was sugar—fruit, sugary cereals, and candy—all of which was completely out of character for me because I had never eaten much candy in my life. My body started craving sugar as a way to counteract the Oxycontin. My body was in a lull from the downers, and as we all remember from childhood and Halloween, sugar gives you a lot of energy. Next I started taking Ambien because I was having trouble sleeping (probably due to all the sugar) and got hooked on that also. At night when the Oxycontin was starting to wear off, I took a couple of Ambien; as I tried to fight against the sleep, I got another kind of high, slipping in and out of consciousness. Then I would finally pass out at five or six in the morning.

My life had become about one thing only: drugs. I was completely depressed because I was taking depressants. I didn't have a lot of conscious thought about grieving the loss of Joan or my dad. I wasn't even thinking about transitioning anymore. My life was miserable. All I thought about was my drugs. I lay in bed counting my pills. In the middle of addiction, I had no ability to see that my life could be better or different. The drugs blocked out everything else that had come before and was still lying underneath. I was in prison, completely enslaved to drugs.

For Christmas 2003, I went to visit my stepmother and siblings in Palm Springs. My doctor was going to be out of town for the holiday, so he gave me a bigger prescription than usual. I remember being in the bedroom where I stayed at my dad's house, counting pills and trying to figure out when to take the extra ones. Time passed vaguely. For New Year's, I went to Hawaii with my mom and brother. I don't think I put on a bathing suit or went to the beach once.

By this time, my prescriptions were so massive that I had to go to a hospital pharmacy to get them filled. Regular pharmacies just didn't carry enough Oxycontin to fill my prescription.

It was now late January 2004. One day, in therapy, I said to Sari, "I don't know why I even come here; I don't like you. I don't know why I am even trying to wean myself off the drugs. I just want to do my drugs. That's all I want to do. I want everyone to stop bugging me and just leave me alone."

"So you want to slowly kill yourself and destroy all the relationships in your life?" Sari asked quietly.

I was waiting to die. I felt nothing.

"Yes," I answered. It was true. I looked at her. For the first time I was being completely honest about exactly what I was doing. I felt no shame, no reluctance about being forthright, no need to pretend anymore.

But suddenly, hearing my words aloud, hearing them for what they were, I experienced a moment of clarity. The denial over how I had been killing myself with drugs suddenly parted like a curtain, and I knew I had to stop.

I drove home not knowing what to do or how to do it, knowing only that I wanted to stop using drugs. I wanted to live. I also knew it would require medical intervention.

Once home, I realized that I couldn't imagine being in my

house not loaded. My friend Garth had just moved into my guest room. We had been working on a screenplay together. So one of the first things I did was tell Garth what was going on and asked him if he would take care of my animals if I had to go away someplace.

Then I called my mom and said, "You're right, I'm on drugs and I need help. Will you please send me to treatment?"

She said yes, of course.

I chose to go to treatment at a facility called Sierra Tucson in Arizona. I liked their approach, which treated not only the addiction itself, but all the issues behind the drug use. I knew I had a lot of sifting through of my life to do. There were many layers of pain. I had a lot of grief issues from the deaths of Joan and my father, and some trauma from the sexual and emotional abuse I suffered in my childhood. I knew that I had a lot of things to work out if I wanted to be sober once and for all. For the first time in my life, I was ready to dig in and do what it took to get better.

I arrived at Sierra Tucson on March 7, 2004. I used drugs for the last time that morning so I wouldn't get dope sick on my way to treatment. I was really terrified about checking myself in to rehab; I was afraid of the pain of the physical withdrawal from opiates—by that time I was taking ten 80-mg Oxycontin a day—and I was also scared of the idea of living my life totally substance-free for the first time in a decade.

When I finally went into withdrawal, it felt like the world tipped upside down. I thought I was dying. My blood pressure went through the roof. I had five tortured days of withdrawal while staying in the hospital area of the rehab facility.

Once the worst of my physical withdrawal was over, I began to integrate myself into the rehabilitation treatment program. Slowly, I felt myself come back to life. It was as if a thawing began to happen, and I started to feel like a human being again. I started to engage with people. I started to laugh. I loved treatment. Community, camaraderie, common goals—all of those feelings appealed to my personality and had always worked for me so well. Even my sex drive came back. I hadn't even masturbated in two years. Everything about me started functioning again.

One of the rituals that I most enjoyed during my stay at Sierra Tucson was the graduation ceremony that took place for those residents who had completed their program. These ceremonies took place twice a week in the amphitheater, and I looked forward to them. Everyone in the community attended, but those who were graduating sat off to the side. Watching others succeed became very empowering. The graduates would go into the rock pit and pick up a rock and throw it into the fire pit—a powerful enactment of throwing their addiction into the fire so that it might burn away.

As my graduation day approached, my mom and brother came up for family week. This was very intense, difficult, and frightening. The program had been pushing me to deal with some of the issues that were hard for me. I had to do a lot of writing and confront my mom about some issues, including Harriet and the feeling that I was a disappointment to her because I was so masculine all my life. I also had the opportunity to make amends to my mom for causing her to worry so much over my drug use. She had been terrified that drug addiction might kill me, and I truly regret having put her through that suffering. The entire experience of family week turned out to be quite healing for both of us.

After thirty days of intensive treatment and sobriety, it was my turn to graduate. I threw my rock of painkillers into the fire pit and got ready to reenter the world. When I left, I was excited and scared. It was the beginning of the second half of my life.

Cher and Chaz at seven months old, 1969

Sonny Bono, Aunt Gee, Chaz, and Cher at Chaz's second birthday party, 1971

Cher and Chaz, 1971

Cher, Sonny, and Chaz, 1971

Kiss fans, Chaz and Elijah Allman, 1978

Best friends, Chaz and Ricky, 1978

Chaz in the seventh grade, 1982

Sonny and Chaz at a tennis
tournament, 1981

Maternal grandmother Georgia
Holt and Chaz, 1983

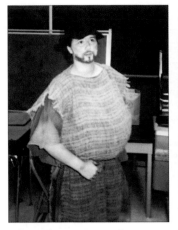

Chaz playing Peter Quince, 1987

Heidi and Chaz at the Oscars, 1987

Chaz, Cher, and Aunt Gee after Cher's Show, 1991

Elijah Allman and Chaz in Malibu, 1992

Joan and Chaz in Maui, 1993

Chaz in Aspen, 1995

Chaz's thirtieth birthday in Long Beach, 1999

Jennifer, Cher, Chaz, and Jennifer's parents after Cher's show in Las Vegas, 2007

Chaz at Christmas in Palm Springs, 2009

Mary Bono Mack, Connie Mack, Chesare Bono, Chaz, and Chianna Bono at Christmas in Palm Springs, 2009

Gina and Chaz reunite, 2010.

Jane (Chaz's sponsor), Chaz, and Lila celebrate at Chaz's MANniversary party, 2010.

Chaz, his goddaughter Anabelle, and Shula, Halloween, 2010

Chaz and Cher at the *Burlesque* premiere, 2010

Chaz and Jennifer at the Sundance Film Festival, 2011

CHAPTER TEN

A Second Chance

After being released from rehab, I wanted to do everything I possibly could to ensure that I maintained my sobriety, so I immediately started outpatient treatment for another four months to stay on track and went back to seeing my therapist Sari. I also attended regular recovery meetings and group gatherings. I needed to make sure I had the most structure possible in my day-to-day life. I went to the outpatient treatment about three days a week, meeting one-on-one with an addiction specialist/counselor. I was also part of different types of support groups—a women's group (ironic, I know), a relapse prevention group, and a relationships-in-recovery group. I wasn't in a relationship then, but I knew I really wanted to be. For a lot of people, relationships are a stressor. Some people haven't ever had sex without drugs or alcohol in their bodies, so even entertaining the idea of a new relationship once sober is daunting, if not dangerous. But I was very lonely and missed sharing my life with somebody. Since I started abusing substances later in life, I had lots of experience being intimate stone-cold sober, so I didn't think that emotional or physical intimacy would jeopardize my recovery. I was used to being in a relationship, and I wanted to meet someone.

But I was still unsure of how to handle the issue of my transition. While I was at Sierra Tucson I started talking to some of the counselors about being transgender and wanting to start my transition. They were very supportive about it, but had also cautioned me to take life slowly. I was aware of how vulnerable people are to making big changes too quickly, or going right back to their old way of life, after rehab—both of which can lead right back into using. In fact, the brain is set up to respond to stress in just this way, especially when the stress is experienced in any kind of environment that is associated with addictive behaviors.

For me, my biggest trigger at home was boredom, so I cocooned myself in recovery-based activities to avoid that. But after a couple of months at home, I felt ready to at least start talking about transitioning. I had been seeing Sari since my return from Sierra Tucson, and she had suggested that I be a year sober before starting to physically transition.

I also reached out to Davis, the FTM therapist whom I had first contacted when I thought I was transgender while with Kathy. Talking with both Davis and Sari helped me to begin to see how fear and confusion about my gender identity was one of the reasons that caused me to use drugs, and I knew I would have to deal with my feelings around this issue.

In preparation for starting my transition, I did take a big step. I mustered my courage to broach the subject with my mom. Quite spontaneously, one day I called her at home and told her I was thinking about needing to transition, explaining that I thought going through with this process was necessary for me to be happy.

Surprisingly, my mom said, "Well, Chas, you are getting

older [I was thirty-five at the time], so you probably shouldn't wait any longer."

Then she suggested that we go to family counseling about it.

My mom didn't seem overjoyed by the idea, but she was more positive than I had anticipated, and I felt relieved. I knew that my transitioning from female to male would be hard for my mother, and I felt a responsibility to include her in my process. I didn't want to make the same mistake as when I had come out to her the first time. This time I wanted to do my best to honor and respect my mother through what I imagined would be a difficult situation for her and something that would require a lot of adjustment of her feelings.

That fall, right before Election Day, the John Kerry campaign contacted me to go to Denver and rally support from the gay and lesbian community. I was more than willing to go—I had done the same thing for Clinton in '96 and was in Florida stumping for Gore the day before the 2000 election. To be frank, I also thought it might be a good opportunity to meet some women. I remember saying to a friend, "They'll appreciate me more in Denver," in reference to the fact that so many of the lesbians in Los Angeles were ultra-feminine (aka lipstick lesbians) and didn't seem interested in those of us who were more butch.

So off I went to Denver, on a mission—well, really two missions.

It was Halloween, and Robin, the woman who was my point person from the campaign, took me to a bunch of clubs and bars, which is where the political events were taking place. I visited with the patrons and then gave a speech on why it was so important to vote for Kerry. It turns out I was right about the gay culture in Denver—it was a lot more diverse. There were more visibly butch lesbians, and not everyone was beautiful and thin as in LA. Robin's boss held a notorious Halloween party every year, and Robin invited me to stay for the party and to crash at her and her partner's house. She also asked if I wanted to be fixed up with a good friend of hers whom she thought I might like. I was totally into it.

At the Halloween party, Robin introduced me to Emily, and we were immediately attracted to each other. She had short red hair, nicely cut, and was five-seven with an average build. She was feminine and attractive, wore makeup, and dressed in women's clothing. There was good chemistry between us, and by the end of the night, we were making out. After being single and celibate for over two years, that was all the fuel I needed. We quickly launched into a long-distance relationship, with us traveling to see each other, when we could, on weekends.

One weekend I was visiting Emily in Denver and we were hanging out watching TV. The guy in the movie we were watching had a beard, and I said something like "I've always wanted to have a beard."

Emily looked at me askance and said, "Well that's weird." She paused and then asked me more directly, "Do you want to be a man?"

I looked at her and said, "Yeah—it's actually something that I'm planning on doing. I've been talking about it for a while in therapy." I was trying to be completely honest with Emily. It felt important to verbalize my true feelings in my current relationship.

Then she replied almost angrily, "I'm a lesbian—I don't want to be with a man. I thought you were butch, which is fine. But I don't want to be with a man."

I started to backpedal right away. "I haven't done anything yet, and I'm not going to do it for sure," I muttered, almost apologetically.

I felt like I was going to have a repeat of what happened with Kathy. I was instantly terrified of losing the relationship. And Emily was making it pretty clear that my transitioning was a deal breaker for her.

My relationship with Emily ended after a few months, though not because I was transgender. Her reaction to the idea, however, scared me, and I got it in my head that I had to choose one or the other: being myself *or* being in a loving relationship.

In therapy I found myself walking a kind of tightrope. On the one hand, I felt that if I transitioned I would feel more comfortable in my own skin; but I knew that as a public figure everyone would know that I had transitioned, and that would make me feel less comfortable out in the world. At that time I was still convinced that if people knew my secret, they would respond to me with open hostility. Looking at it now, I realize it sounds a bit narcissistic, but at the time I still really cared what other people thought of me. I couldn't conceive that anyone could possibly understand or accept me if I transitioned.

Though I thought I was ready to begin the transitioning process after rehab, it was becoming clear that I really wasn't. I was convinced that if I transitioned I would be alone and misunderstood forever, so I came up with another plan: I was going to let myself be as male as I wanted, but not go ahead with any kind of physical change. I had never let myself be free enough to do even this. I thought it might work—that this kind of compromise might be enough. I was trying to embrace and integrate the man inside me, without hormonal or surgical intervention. In reality nothing on the outside changed all that much. I think I may have cut my hair a bit shorter. The change was more internal. Up until that point, I had fought against my natural masculinity to a certain extent, feeling that, as a biological female, this part of me was wrong, or a mistake. Now I was going to try to make peace with it. I also stopped seeing Davis, my transgender therapist—another indication of my intention to drop the idea of transitioning altogether.

In March of that year, 2005, my favorite cat, Stinky, died. This loss made me feel more lonely than ever. When I was doing drugs and isolating myself from everyone, it was often Stinky that kept me going. I took her everywhere with me—as if she were a dog. When I was still using, and had to consciously summon reasons to live, one of them was that no one would take as good care of Stinky as I did. Unfortunately, Stinky had heart defects that I wasn't aware of, and after going into congenital heart failure, she died within a month, two days after my first sober anniversary.

Right after this, my mom again offered to help me buy a nicer house. When we talked, the subject of my transition didn't come up, and it wouldn't for another three years. I had sold my old house at a good profit (right before the market dropped again); my mom matched my half, and we bought a new house together, keeping it in trust so I could keep my address private. That summer I finally had my uterus removed to deal with, once and for all, my chronic painful endometriosis. Now truly sober, I was very limited in what I could use for pain management. My vulnerability to pain medicines was further complicated by a genetic blood disorder that I had been diagnosed with in my early teens that affects my blood's ability to clot. After a class of anti-inflammatory medication that I had been using to manage the endometrial pain was recalled, I decided to have the one surgery that could alleviate my pain issue once and for all—a partial hysterectomy. It was finally an end to a lifetime of misery.

One summer night after going out to dinner with a friend and her new girlfriend, we came back to my house to hang out in the pool and I asked them if they knew anyone to set me up with. I had been planning a barbecue for that following week, and my friends brought along Jenny.

It was August 15, 2005, right after Jenny's thirtieth birthday. I felt really shy about meeting her. I was in the middle of cooking when she arrived, so I went over and said, "Hi, I'm Chaz," and then went back to the grill. (Ever since I was sober, I had been referring to myself as Chaz.)

After everyone ate, half the people left. It was starting to get late, and soon it was just Jenny and me under the gazebo, talking. At the time, my ex-girlfriend Kathy was living in my guesthouse, but she had gone to sleep. Jenny and I were pretty much by ourselves.

As soon as we started talking, we hit it off. It was effortless. I thought Jenny was really funny, smart, and quirky, and I liked her as a person right away. Neither of us had a love-at-first-sight moment, but in my experience those types of relationships usually don't end up working out, for one reason or another.

Jenny had been born and raised in Riverdale, New York, and had moved to Los Angeles in 1998. She had recently ended a difficult relationship and moved to Venice Beach to take a break from the Hollywood scene and try to find herself again. She stopped wearing makeup, wore her hair in a ponytail, and didn't seem exactly interested in her appearance. This is how she looked that day at my house. (I'd learn later from her that this was very conscious on her part—her previous relationship had been very destructive, leaving her self-esteem at an all-time low.)

Like me, Jenny had recently celebrated her first year of sobriety. I was interested in her, but I wanted to take any new relationship more slowly this time. I really wanted to get to know Jenny before I made the mistake of making our relationship sexual before either of us was ready. Though we seemed to have a special bond, I didn't want to put undue stress on getting to know each other by immediately making our relationship physical. I also didn't want to get too attached if things weren't going to work out. I was trying to be a little wiser about relationships in my thirties.

We got into my Jacuzzi, which probably sent the wrong signal. I think she was waiting for me to make a move, but I didn't. We did stay up very late talking in an effortless and engaging manner.

The next morning I woke up realizing that I really liked her.

I called her and asked to meet her that night. In the next week, we went out every night but one. Within a couple of weeks, she was staying with me. She eventually gave up her Venice apartment. She took out a small studio rental in West Holly-wood just in case, but essentially we were living together.

Some habits are really hard to change.

I soon discovered that Jenny had never been with a woman as masculine as me. Most of the women she had been involved with were straight or bisexual, and though she enjoyed the dynamics and company of men, sometimes more than women, and the feeling of safety and security they brought to the relationship, she explained that she never felt fully in sync with most men. She also felt that she was more sexually attracted to women, although she was in fact attracted to both sexes.

This is where bisexuality is difficult: people often feel pressure to choose between genders. Of course, you don't have to choose, but Jenny felt she did. Sexually she was slightly more attracted to women, but some aspects of maleness attracted her, too. Neither gender had ever been completely fulfilling for her . . . until she met me. I don't think she ever imagined having both those needs met by someone who was transgender.

But I'm getting ahead of myself.

Right from the start, my relationship with Jenny was qualita-tively different from any other relationship I had had. (Perhaps with the exception of Joan—though even then, I was so young and I can't really say I knew myself at all.) But as I did with Joan, I felt very comfortable and compatible with Jenny, with a clear sense that she liked me as I was. She totally got my masculinity and never tried to get me to change or to be more feminine.

My ex-girlfriend Kathy was still living in my guesthouse, which soon became problematic. When Jenny and I got serious, about a month or so into our relationship, Kathy started to become hostile toward her. She started telling me lies about Jenny, and giving Jenny reasons to question me. Kathy even went so far as to tell Jenny that the only reason she and I weren't together any longer was because I thought I was transgender.

This happened about a month into our relationship. Of course, I had been planning on sharing this information about myself with Jenny, but I wanted to get to know her a little better first. In the past, when this subject had come up with women I was dating, it hadn't been received very well, so there was a big part of me that was afraid I'd lose her as soon as she found out about my truth.

Though it was clearly Kathy's intention to scare Jenny off with this news, it didn't work. Instead it opened up a dialogue between me and Jenny that needed to happen, and, thankfully, brought us even closer.

Jenny came and found me in the bathroom getting ready for bed. She told me what Kathy had said to her and asked me if that was true. I told Jenny that it was the truth and then shared with her my whole history.

I explained that I thought I was transgender, but that at the moment I wasn't ready to begin the actual transitioning process. I was simply trying to let myself be who I really was, as masculine as I'd always wanted to be. I remember Jenny asking how it was working out for me. I explained to her that at the moment I was feeling okay about it, but that could change. I then explained that I couldn't guarantee I would not transition in the future.

Then I added, "The idea of growing old as a woman is so

repugnant to me that at some point later in life I will probably have to transition."

Jenny seemed nonplussed.

But in saying these words aloud, I realized that I had let part of me go to sleep. I knew the desire to transition wasn't gone, and I knew I hadn't "stopped" being transgender. Ever since the brief relationship with Emily, and after experiencing her viscerally negative reaction to the idea, I'd been afraid to see or read anything having to do with being transgender, so afraid of awakening the sleeping giant within me.

I had avoided going to Outfest that year, Los Angeles's gay and lesbian film festival, because I didn't want to be tempted to see any more films on the topic. Before this time, I constantly read books about transgender issues and people's real life stories, seeking out any information that would help me wrap my head around how people dealt with the situation. At previous Outfests I had seen some amazing documentaries about FTMs that I had really connected with, but now I was afraid of that connection. I was very consciously avoiding anything having to do with the topic.

I remember thinking of my desire to transition almost as a disease, wanting it to lie dormant, hoping it wouldn't come out of remission and wreak havoc on my life. Like the comic book character Bruce Banner, my being transgender felt like having the Incredible Hulk ready to explode from within me and ruin my life.

I didn't realize that I had it all backward, that being a transgender man was my real identity, and that my fear itself was the angry green monster preventing me from truly being myself and being happy.

Jenny and I were settling in, and with eighteen months of sobriety under my belt, I began to feel like it was time to figure out what I was going to do with my career. My last book, which was not very successful, had come out in 2002, and I hadn't worked at all since then. I really enjoyed the activist work I had done in the gay and lesbian community, but I no longer felt that was an option. After all, I knew I wasn't a lesbian; I was a closeted transgender person, which made going back to working in the GLBT community feel totally hypocritical—especially if I couldn't work on behalf of the "T" part of that acronym.

Then that fall, fortune fell into my lap when the producers of a VH1 reality show called *Celebrity Fit Club* came calling. I had always been pretty anti–reality TV, but I thought this show would be a good launching pad for me and perhaps open me up to a different kind of work on television. After being assured over and over again by the producers that their intention was to create a show that would help and inspire people and not be exploitive, I decided to sign on.

I was being paid to lose weight. I had always had a propensity for gaining weight. I didn't take after my mother's side of the family, who are all naturally thin; instead, I take after my dad's side of the family. During my years of drug addiction, the downers literally slowed down my metabolism, and because of that, coupled with poor eating habits and little physical activity, I had put on quite a bit of weight. What could be wrong with now being paid to lose that weight?

I must admit, though, that in the back of my mind, I also

thought that if I lost weight and built more muscle, then maybe I would feel more comfortable in my body. It had always been hard for me to motivate myself to lose weight and regularly exercise because I was so disconnected from my physical body. I mean, no matter what kind of shape I was in, I always hated the female reflection looking back at me from the mirror. Anytime I tried to lose weight, I had to approach it from a purely health point of view. For most people, focusing on how they look keeps them motivated. For me, no matter how much weight I lost, I would just see a thinner body that I hated. I thought this time might be different.

But doing *Celebrity Fit Club* turned out to be very frustrating. In my opinion, the creators of the show didn't actually teach us how to lose weight. Since this *was* television after all, the producers wanted to give the viewers dramatic results, which meant they expected us to lose large amounts of weight very quickly. We were under tremendous pressure. We were even encouraged to not do any kind of muscle-building activity, since muscle is very dense, and adding muscle, even when you're losing fat, doesn't lead to good results on the scale. You might be losing inches, but your weight won't always change. The whole program was focused only on strict dieting and hard-core cardio exercise.

In the third week, I plateaued. Another contestant weighed in that week and he had lost a significant amount of weight. So I asked him what he was doing and he told me that he had preordered the Zone Diet! So that's what we all ended up doing, too. And it worked. I was probably on eleven to twelve hundred calories a day, and I was in a foul mood all the time because I was constantly hungry—but weight came off.

The show shot for a total of twelve weeks. I kept losing weight through the entire shoot schedule—I ended up losing twenty-five pounds all together during those three months, but most of it in those last eight weeks on the Zone Diet.

Combining weight loss and the need for drama in television is at odds, in my opinion. Losing weight is about changing eating and exercise habits, something you have to do slowly and safely, and the problem for me with a lot of reality competition shows is that all the producers care about is trying to stir up as much drama as possible. None of us were taking the competition seriously. My castmates were great—and I enjoyed the group of people I was working with. We wouldn't divide ourselves into two teams or pit ourselves against one another; we just wanted to get through the process as peacefully as possible. We all wanted to spark our careers and get healthy. This was not, of course, what VH1 had in mind. The producers of the show weren't focused on helping us get healthier—in fact, quite the opposite. The activities felt reckless at times. We literally didn't feel safe.

When the show premiered, I would read the blogs and what people were writing about me—things like "She looks like a guy." This didn't hurt my feelings at all. I'd just say to myself, "Yeah, I do."

To me, this was an all-too-familiar indication of how disturbing gender variance is to most people. Other than that, I got very good responses about how I came off on the show. People generally seemed to like and relate to me. I remember my mom even telling me that several people had told her how much they enjoyed watching me during that season.

After the show aired in January 2006, I tried to use it as a springboard to get more work. Doing *Celebrity Fit Club* had one positive impact: I realized that I liked being in front of the camera and was reminded that I could be compelling on the small screen. Even though this show wasn't the greatest vehicle, I did get positive reviews and responses to my work. So I hired a publicist, and Dina, my lawyer, also tried to spark my career. I had an idea for a loosely scripted show (similar in style and format to what Larry David does on *Curb Your Enthusiasm*), and we set up some meetings with agents. But no one wanted me to do anything but more straight reality TV, which is not what I wanted. I also met with a handful of TV production companies, and again the only type of show they were interested in producing for me was some type of reality show. I was still pretty anti–reality TV then. I have since broadened my outlook on this television genre and believe that there are some truly creative, entertaining, and even beneficial reality shows now being made.

I then wrote a treatment for a video game with a friend, who was a film producer, but I soon found that industry to be completely impenetrable. I have been into gaming since I was a little kid. My dad had a pinball machine and the original video game, Pong, in his basement while I was growing up. Later my mom became obsessed with the game Pac-Man and we had the tabletop version in our house. I used to love to go to the arcade as a child, and got even more into gaming when Nintendo launched their home system in the late eighties. I enjoy playing all different types of video games. Now my favorites are action role-playing games, which let me build a character of my own creation and then spend time in an alternate reality and fantasy setting.

I could also be male when gaming, creating an avatar that looked like I'd always wished I did, with big muscles and lots of facial hair.

We had worked tirelessly on our game proposal and come up with a very detailed treatment for our RPG's, or Role Playing Game's, story line, but unlike film and television, where story ideas and scripts often come into a production company from independent writers, in the gaming industry all of the intellectual properties are developed in-house; they don't want to hear about fresh, new ideas from outside. My attorney also tried to help me shop the game treatment, but we quickly found out that making any headway was going to be next to impossible.

Finally, Garth, my friend from high school, and I landed a development deal from a gay television network called HERE, to write a script for a TV movie. We worked on that for the next twelve months. We had previously written the script together while I was still using drugs, but for obvious reasons hadn't done anything with it. It needed a lot of work, but HERE seemed to see that the story, which was something I'd conceived, had potential. I had originally plotted out the story when I was still working at the *Advocate*. I interviewed a lesbian filmmaker who told me that she had recently fallen in love with a man, and that everyone in her life, her friends and family, became really upset about it. That story got me thinking about how sexuality is very fluid for many people, like Jenny, and wondering why our culture is still uncomfortable with this idea. Though I myself have never been sexually attracted to men, I have always thought that people who can fall in love with an individual and not a gender are very evolved. So our script, *In the Name of Love*, was about two old female friends, one straight and one gay; and then the lesbian falls in love with a man and the straight woman falls in love with a woman. The story follows how these changes impact their lives and friendship.

By April 2007, after we had rewritten the script several times for HERE, the network decided not to make it into a film. I started to get disheartened and depressed. I was frustrated that my career had stalled, and I had no idea of what to do next.

When I got sober, I had made a conscious decision that I was going to be happy and grateful for everything in my life. I had spent so many years being truly miserable that this was an easy decision to make, and in spite of some true challenges, an easy promise to keep. A very wise friend of mine with over forty years of sobriety told me that, when newly out of rehab, it is impossible to relapse if you live your life with an attitude of gratitude. My life continued to move along, and in spite of the fact that things certainly didn't feel easy or smooth, I still knew that I had a lot to be grateful for: my sobriety, my relationship with Jenny, our home and animals, to name a few.

But Jenny seemed to sense something was wrong. She'd often say to me, "Chaz, you've got to do something. All you're doing is playing video games."

I knew she was right. I didn't want to do drugs, and I truly was trying to be as happy as possible. But the career stalls and disappointments were getting to me. In hindsight I realize not transitioning was one thing that was really stopping me from moving forward in life.

During all of this, my discomfort with my physical body really started to reemerge. I had tried for the past couple years to be male, but in my female body. The truth is that I just wasn't female and couldn't feel comfortable, no matter how manly I acted, in that body. I was still terrified to transition, so I came up with yet another plan—I decided to move forward with top surgery. At the time, I thought I could have top surgery and no one would notice. That way, I wouldn't have to come out to the world as trans. I decided this during the summer, which was the one time of year that I just couldn't ignore the fact that I had breasts. I have a pool. I love to swim, but putting on a bathing suit top always affected me: I couldn't ignore my breasts. I couldn't just wear a baggy shirt to swim. I had to see my breasts all summer long.

So I talked to Jenny about this new idea, and she seemed unfazed and supportive. I had long ago asked her to not touch my breasts while we were having sex. She knew of my discomfort with that part of my body. So the plan was set: as soon as I had some extra money, I would go ahead with top surgery.

In the fall I got offered a job to do a Q&A, on various GLBT issues, on a cruise ship for the lesbian vacation company Olivia. I thought to myself, *Okay—here is the money for the top surgery.* The surgery cost roughly the same amount as what I was being paid to do the cruise. The irony of the situation was that Olivia cruises are for lesbians, and part of the proceeds from that cruise was going toward breast cancer research. Here I was going to use the money I made there to have my own breasts removed. I felt really uncomfortable. I didn't move forward at that time, but not only because of this irony. I also had a realization in therapy with Sari that I was deluding myself into thinking that I could do something like have top surgery without the press finding out about it. I still wasn't ready to come out as transgender. So I continued to wait.

One night my sponsor Jane called me and told me she was watching this amazing show that Barbara Walters was doing on transgender kids, and Jenny and I turned it on. I remember thinking this show was probably safe for me to watch because it was focused on children. I wouldn't relate to it in the same way I would if the show was about adult transgender people.

But during the show, Jenny said sweetly to me, "Oh, babe, is that how you felt when you were a kid?"

I was kind of shocked. I said, "Yes." Inside, I was freaking out. The monster was coming back to life.

A short time later, I went to a meeting where I ran into a trans male named Luke, whom I had met before he transitioned. He wasn't a good friend; I knew him from when Kathy and I were together and we'd see him at parties. He was about ten to fifteen years older than me and had been as butch as he could be as a woman. I had heard through the sober grapevine that he was transitioning, but I hadn't seen him in a few years.

When I saw him at this meeting, he was a completely transformed person. He looked amazing. It wasn't so much his physical transformation—yes, he had lost a lot of weight, and he also had facial hair, and there was a spring in his step. But what I saw more than anything was happiness in every ounce of his being.

And then the monster started to roar.

CHAPTER ELEVEN

Decision

The combination of seeing Luke so clearly fulfilled and happy in his new body, and my realization that I wasn't going to be able to have top surgery without anyone noticing led me to one conclusion: top surgery wasn't going to solve my bigger problem. The truth was obvious: I was going to have to transition. And I was going to have to come out again. I was terrified.

For the next year, in every therapy session with Sari, all I talked about was my need to transition, and the fact that I was too scared to do so. Week after week I would discuss my litany of fears, referring back to my catalogue of dreads and frightening fantasies. Some of the fears had dissipated; some had actually come true. New fears would appear, and some would remain the same. I was afraid that Jenny would leave me, that my mom and the rest of my family would stop talking to me, that I would no longer feel like me, that my friends would desert me, that the public would think I was crazy or a freak, that the gay and lesbian community would think of me as a traitor, and so on and so on. But unlike earlier when I was with Kathy, I could no longer bury my desire to transition. I could no longer sublimate it by allowing myself to be as masculine as possible. I knew that the only way I was ever going to feel happy or complete was if I transitioned.

I was so stuck. Stuck in purgatory. Before this point, I had given myself a list of "to-dos" that had to happen in order to transition: first, I had to get sober, then I would try to be masculine, then I would just get my breasts cut off. Nothing had worked. The delusion was broken by watching Barbara Walters's special on transgender youth, and running into Luke.

It was all too clear: I was who I was. I had to do what I had to do. I was paralyzed with fear.

During this period, my reality had become so difficult for me that I spent as much time as I could in an alternate one. Gaming became a new drug for me, something that I could do to alleviate the pain and just zone out. When I was gaming, I could become the strong, handsome, courageous hero conquering foes and slaying dragons, instead of feeling like the weakest, most impotent coward in the world, which was how I saw myself.

For the first time, I started writing about the pain and confusion that I was feeling. The following excerpt is a great example of my state of mind then.

January 2008

> I have heard the saying "We are only as sick as our secrets" used time and time again in the recovery programs I belong to, and I've slowly come to understand that while this is true, my spirituality is on life support. I have a secret, a big fucking doozy of a secret that I have held in for a long time. Even as I sit here, I still don't know if I'm ready to confess my secret publicly.

However as a public figure that's shared everything else about myself with the world, anything less than a public admission seems like a big fat lie.

So here goes, I'm not a lesbian. I'm not a straight woman either. The truth is I have never felt like very much of any kind of woman. What I believe I am is a transgender person. I use the word "person" because as of now I have not done anything to physically transition into being or becoming male or more male, and because I have always been uncomfortable using gender specific pronouns in reference to myself. Before I go back to the beginning and try to explain how I have come to identify as a transgender, I want elucidate why it's important to me now to write this all down.

Because I feel like a liar and a fraud. I feel like I've been "passing" as a lesbian for years and pretending to be something I'm not. It's because due to the all-consuming fear I have experienced since I came to this realization, I find myself back in the dark but safe closet I thought I closed the door on forever twelve years ago. Finally it is because I think it might be time to, once again, leave the darkness and step into the light.

To date, nothing has terrified me more than coming out as a transgender. There is a huge knot in my stomach right now just writing this alone at my desk. The fear of rejection from my family, friends, recovery sisters and brothers, gay, lesbian and bisexual community, and the gay-friendly straight community, has prevented me from being true to myself and helping other transgender people who are suffering as I am.

In 1998 I wrote a book called *Family Outing* that was a coming out guide for gays and lesbians and their parents. I believed then and I believe now that coming out of the closet is the most personally healing and politically empowering action that we can do for ourselves and our community. Yet I have let fear conquer my convictions, silence my voice, and render me impotent as an activist. Unfortunately I have no idea how to overcome this fear that imprisons me in a continual state of inactivity. I think about transitioning countless times throughout the day. Sometimes I'm filled with an overwhelming sense of well-being imagining my body changing on the outside to better reflect how I feel inside. Other times when I see my girlfriend's face, anxiety casting a dark shadow over it at the prospect of my transitioning, or when I imagine what I would be putting my mother through if I actually did this, I decide there is no way I can ever go through with a transition. Every day this battle rages inside my head and every day that it does is another day in which fear is my master. The worst of it is that these days have strung together into years, close to a decade, and I am no closer to a resolution. It is my inability to tame my fear and take action so I can do what I feel is right for me that causes me so much frustration.

I hope that writing about the feelings, philosophy, and history of my self-discovery as a transgender individual will lead me to make a decision once and for all. God, please help me to man up, literally, and take the greatest adventure of my life or let me put aside all this nonsense about transitioning, never to be plagued by it again. Amen.

I now started discussing the subject with Jenny not just in the abstract, but as a definitive reality. I tried to explain to her what I was going through and how I was feeling. I wanted to know what she thought she would do if I transitioned. I asked her if she'd leave me. I asked her if she felt she would be less attracted to me. I was terrified to lose her. Imagining my body transformed and finally losing its femaleness made me push through my fears to talk about my need to transition.

When Jenny's response to me was positive, I'd feel positive and hopeful that together we would figure out how to manage my transition. In those conversations, she told me how much she loved me and that she believed we could get through anything I needed to do. But when Jenny gave me any hesitancy, I would back off and drop the subject, only to bring it up again a month or so later and wait and see how she reacted. When she seemed more positive then, I would push the subject; when she gave me a negative reaction, I'd back off—it became a bad form of emotional ping-pong.

Sometimes, Jenny even got a bit mean. "You're never going to be a real man—you'll never look like a real guy." This hurt.

One time she said bluntly, "I don't think I could handle it," adding, "I certainly couldn't do it sober." She knew this part of the equation worried me, especially since during the summer of 2006 she had relapsed. She'd been waiting tables at the time, and one of her waiter friends would sometimes give her Vicodin. Eventually, one night she stayed out late drinking and partying with friends from the restaurant. By the time she got home, I was a nervous wreck and was about to check a nearby emergency room. When I realized she had relapsed, I freaked and kicked her out of the house, telling her that she couldn't come back until she went into treatment. I was really afraid of losing her and the relationship, but I also expected her to stay clean if we were together.

Then I began attending a support group for friends and families of alcoholics and learned that Jenny was what is called a "periodic" substance abuser. Until then, I hadn't quite understood my part in the situation. The fact that I was in recovery got in my way; my views were very narrow and black-and-white. I thought that as an addict myself, I couldn't possibly be in a relationship with somebody who was also a substance abuser and not 100 percent sober herself. I finally came to accept that as long as Jenny's drinking didn't jeopardize my own sobriety, which it didn't, I could be all right whether she was sober or not. I also learned to mind my own business and stay out of her recovery program, which made both of our lives a lot more peaceful. As much as I wanted Jenny to stay clean, I couldn't force her to do what I wanted. She had to want it for herself.

But the repercussions from Jenny's relapse would surface when we felt tension, especially when we were going back and forth about my desire to transition.

Both extremes of Jenny's responses were, of course, valid: one side of her was rational and loving; the other was completely terrified.

When I finally showed Jenny pictures from the Web site of the doctor I was thinking of using for my top surgery, she told me the chests were ugly. It became clear that she hadn't really understood what top surgery was all about. She'd had in mind a radical breast reduction. Top surgery was 100 percent breast removal.

I was equally scared of what going through with a transition would do to my mother. Though I had told her that I felt ready to transition, and needed to do so in order to be happy, I couldn't be sure how she would react when I actually began the process. And I was loath to put anything between us. Oddly enough, during the preceding year, my mom had started coming with me to my regular support meeting for family and friends of alcoholics— the meetings I had started attending after Jenny's relapse the summer before. My mom had her own reasons for attending these meetings, and they ended up bringing us closer.

I had been working hard to let go of some of the resentment I still felt toward my mom for how I was raised. By coming to those meetings, she was making an effort to have a relationship with me. We both were putting a lot of energy into our relationship then, and it was paying off. For the first time in a very long time, we were really close. We were starting to get know each other as adults, past all my drug addiction drama and my childhood resentments.

The thought of breaking this new closeness by telling her that I was going to finally start my transition made me feel like I had more to lose than ever. I also knew that going through my transition was going to bring media scrutiny on her, and give the tabloids another reason to bother her. This made me feel incredibly guilty.

Then one day in my regular Friday therapy appointment, I was talking with Sari about transitioning, describing my usual parade of fears, and Sari said, "You realize that this is about control, or the lack thereof, right?" Referring to the recovery process, she then said, "Chaz, remember your first step: you are powerless over others."

I knew exactly what she was talking about: you are powerless over the reactions of others—how other people will feel, react to you. I knew what Sari meant: that I had to start making choices in my life that were based on me, my needs, my desires, regardless of how they might impact the people in my life.

This inevitability cut to my core; putting myself first was something I had never done.

And then, much like when I came to the realization about my drug abuse and felt the impetus to stop using, I experienced another incredible moment of clarity about myself. I understood for the first time that I couldn't focus on how others were going to react if I transitioned. I could not possibly control their reactions, their feelings, their behaviors toward me. I had been so consumed with not upsetting anyone, but I could not continue deferring my own needs. Now I accepted that these people were all adults. It wasn't my job to make them okay; they had to make themselves okay with me. Which meant that the only person really in my way was myself.

I drove home from therapy single-minded. When I walked in the door, Jenny was sitting on the couch. She turned and asked me how therapy was and what we'd talked about. This was not a very typical question for her, I might add.

With surprise, I looked at her and then I told her about my conversation with Sari.

"Oh, that's great!" Jenny replied. "Your therapist just tells you to do whatever is good for you, regardless of how it impacts anyone else!" She was upset and I instantly felt myself getting nervous. But I stood my ground.

"That's not fair. You know I've been struggling with this for years—how can you say I don't care?" I tried again to explain how much pain I was in, living in this state of limbo, and how tortured I felt inside by not taking steps toward transition.

"Your pain? The world does not revolve around you, Chaz!" Jenny said, almost spitefully.

We were both well versed in recovery lingo, so I responded defensively with "You know better than anyone that I have to stop taking care of everyone else's needs and start taking care of my own."

Then Jenny launched into a litany of mean comments: "You're never going to look like a real man. Transgender people never really look like the sex they are trying to be."

I felt anger rising in my throat.

"That's just not true," I replied emphatically. "Most FTMs pass really well."

Jenny continued, "Your chest will never look like a real man's chest. You will have bad scars and the nipples won't be in the right place."

Fuck you, I thought. *Here we go again. The same game of chess.* Jenny was pushing my buttons, specifically my fears about never really looking like a man.

This time I was not going to retreat with an apology. In the past my usual response would have been, "We don't have to talk about this now, baby; don't worry, nothing is happening tomorrow."

I moved my men forward on the chessboard against hers. "I don't care how good my chest will look; as long as my breasts are finally gone, I'll be happy."

More somberly, Jenny went on. "I know that if you don't transition you'll end up becoming miserable and depressed. I also know that if you do transition, then I'll become the one who becomes miserable and depressed. But you do what you have to do. I'll just have to start taking Valium to deal with it."

"What, are you crazy?" I shouted, infuriated that she would use the relapse card.

She knew how important her sobriety was to me. She was relying on my very old habit of putting her pain before my own.

But instead of reassuring her that I wouldn't start my transition unless she was okay with it, I became enraged by what I perceived as a blatant attempt to control me by playing the martyr. I had clearly experienced a breakthrough.

I exploded, and I never explode, ever. All the pain and frustration from years of suppressing who I really was had finally erupted into a mighty roar; I found myself screaming—I don't think I was even saying words. It turned into a primal scream, howling and banging my fists against the wall.

I then reached such a heightened state of rage that I knew I had to leave the house.

I saw my whole life flash before my eyes: the issues I had been dealing with forever. That I was a man. That I always bowed to others and not my own needs.

Jenny was in a state of shock. I was always the calm one. I had never raised my voice, never mind screamed. Yet here I was on the verge of being violent.

So I got in my car and left.

After driving for a few blocks, I called my close friend Ginger, who lived nearby. She told me to come to her house. As soon as I heard Ginger's calming voice, I started to feel a bit better, so I called Jenny from my car, on the way to Ginger's house, to let her know that I was okay and was sorry that I had scared her.

I spent several hours at Ginger's talking with her and letting her help me calm down.

A few hours later, I went home. I knew Jenny wasn't going to be there, because she'd made plans to see a friend that night before our fight. Emotionally exhausted, I went to sleep.

The next day when Jenny and I talked, the air between us was palpably different. Everything seemed changed. We both now understood the severity of the situation for me and that it no longer could be ignored.

Over the next few days, in the wake of my outburst, we kept talking, deciding that the best way to handle my decision to transition was to begin couples therapy. We chose to start seeing my old therapist Davis, who, as an FTM himself, would be able to answer the questions that Jenny had about the transition process. Also, Jenny had never met another transgender man before, and I hoped that if she got to spend some time with Davis, any misconception or prejudice she might have about FTMs would be alleviated.

The first session we had with Davis was very hard and Jenny cried a lot, but it was also when I began to believe that Jenny and I could get through this process together.

It meant surrendering control. It meant taking a leap of faith that Jenny, and my mother, would eventually get to where I was, as well.

My next step was to talk to a medical doctor. When I shared my decision to transition with Dr. Stephens, she was completely supportive. She even confided in me that she had four transgender patients, three MTFs and one FTM, and that as an endocrinologist she managed all their hormone therapy. Her one request was that I lose ten more pounds (I had already lost fifteen pounds since the beginning of the year, when I had made a resolution to exercise more often and adopt healthier eating habits) before starting testosterone, as it can raise blood pressure and cholesterol levels. I left Dr. Stephens's office elated.

With my doctor on board, there was only one more major obstacle to overcome. I had to tell my mother what I intended to do. How do you tell your parent that you really are going to change your gender? How do you tell her that the abstract notion is now a reality? That you are not going to be her daughter anymore but her son?

I was very stressed, to say the least.

The Saturday after my appointment with Dr. Stephens I saw my mom at a morning support group meeting and asked her if I could come by her apartment later to talk. We made plans to meet later that evening.

When I got home and told Jenny that I was going to my mom's that night to tell her that I was finally ready to go through with my transition, Jenny became visibly nervous.

"There's no way your mom is going to be cool with this, Chaz. Are you sure you want to tell her?"

But as Jenny and I continued to talk, I began to feel that Jenny's anxiety was based more on her own fears rather than any true insight into my mother's psyche. Jenny was still struggling greatly with her own acceptance of my transition and was scared of her own parents' reaction. She also knew that if my mom accepted my choice, then there was no stopping me.

During the short drive over to my mom's place, I felt surprisingly calm. I had been putting off this conversation for months, waiting for the right moment, and I felt with absolute clarity that the moment was now. As part of the recovery philosophy that I have adopted into my life, I try to follow God's will above my own. As you can imagine, differentiating between my will and God's will is a little difficult. An explanation I have heard many times at meetings is that when you are following God's will, it should feel easy, versus your own, which will feel difficult, like forcing a square peg into a round hole. With everything about my transition starting to fall into place, talking to my mom that day felt easy.

When I got to my mom's apartment, we sat down together on her overstuffed living room couch with a view of all of West Los Angeles. After quickly catching up on some family news, I said to my mom, "You know that I have been dealing with issues over my gender identity for a long time now, and I have decided to transition."

"All right," she said almost too easily.

She was so calm, she seemed Zen-like to me.

My mom paused and then said, "How is Jenny doing with all this?"

I explained to her that it was really hard for Jenny and that she had a lot of fears about my transitioning. "She's extremely anxious that the tabloids are going to write horrible stories about me and invade our privacy. I think she's also concerned that her parents will not understand."

"Well, that's reasonable," my mom said.

"We started going to couples counseling and that's helping— both of us."

"What about your own fears with transitioning?" she asked, logically.

I explained that at one point they were so numerous that they paralyzed me. I was afraid of the media's backlash, public criticism, excommunication from the GLBT community, and Jenny leaving.

"It's taken me years, Mom, but I finally realize that I'm powerless over how other people react to anything in my life, including changing my gender. I just can't let what other people think stop me from doing what I need to do."

"Good," she said, smiling.

It was true. I had reached a place where I had faith that no matter what happened, in the end, I was going to be okay.

Awkwardly, I then said to my mom, "I am afraid about the effect of the testosterone, that it will make me feel mentally and emotionally different than I feel now. I'm also kind of worried about having an increased sex drive."

I looked up and my mom was laughing. "Why are you concerned about having an increased sex drive? When that happens, it will just feel natural, like a part of you."

Shyly, I said, "Sex for me has never felt like something I needed but rather something I wanted. I'm afraid an increased desire for sex is going to make me feel out of control."

Still laughing, my mom responded, "What, you think you're just going to want to jump women on the street?"

"I don't know," I said, trying to smile.

"Oh, don't be ridiculous," my mom answered, and then we were both laughing.

We spent the next couple of hours catching up on a myriad of different subjects having nothing to do with my transition. I left my mom's apartment at eleven that night feeling like an enormous boulder had been lifted off my shoulders.

CHAPTER TWELVE

Transformations

In most ways, my decision to transition turned my life around. My relationship, my health, my decision to return to school all followed, moving in a positive direction. I knew without a doubt that I had made one of the best, and hardest earned, decisions of my life.

As I headed into the fall, I was feeling physically stronger and stronger. I had lost some weight, lowered my cholesterol, and in general started taking better care of myself. I was really motivated for the first time in my life to become more fit, because I finally had the opportunity to look and feel the way I'd always wanted. The one healthy habit that I was able to maintain from doing *Celebrity Fit Club* was exercising on a regular basis, and now, with this new incentive, I began to really step that up.

Jenny and I were also in a really good place. The couples therapy had made a big difference in our relationship in general, especially concerning her comfort level with my upcoming transition. In therapy, Jenny had had the chance to talk about and process her fears about me transitioning. Jenny had to work out whether she could be involved with me if I was a man, and be attracted to me as a man. Though I didn't understand it at the time, Jenny's issues were all based on her fears, as mine were based on my own fears. She was afraid that she was losing the person that she fell in love with, of being judged by others for dating a transgender person, and she was completely terrified of having to tell her parents.

For Jenny the hardest thing was telling her parents about my transition. When she finally told them, they reacted very lovingly, which made Jenny finally feel at peace with my decision.

For Christmas that year we stayed in LA and went to my mom's house. I hadn't seen much of her since the summer, when we'd sat down and talked about my decision to move forward with the transition. She'd been busy; I'd been busy.

On Christmas Day, gathered with Jenny and the rest of my family at my mom's home in Malibu, my mother felt distant, and I felt something was off between her and me.

While we were all hanging out, Jimmy, my brother's best friend, asked me what was going on in my life and about my plans for the New Year.

I told him vaguely that I actually had big plans.

And then he said, "Oh, are you going to transition?"

I realized then that he had already heard this information.

"Yes," I said, and looked over at my mom. She had this scared look on her face—one that hadn't been there in July.

I knew something had changed.

A few days after Christmas, I got a call from my mom's assistant, saying that my mom wanted to have a meeting with my therapist Sari, Dr. Stephens, and the rest of our family (my aunt, brother, and grandmother). I sensed a certain amount of urgency to the meeting, so I called everyone right away and then got back to my mom's assistant to set up the appointment.

But days, and then weeks, went by without me hearing back from my mom.

I called my mom's assistant again, because Sari was holding the appointment time.

She told me that the time didn't work for my mom. "We'll call you when we know what's happening."

Suddenly the urgency was gone, and I felt like a nag for pushing the issue.

Another week or so went by. At some point, I got a call from my mom's assistant saying that Dr. Stephens wanted a meeting with me, my mom, and Sari. It was almost the middle of January by this point.

Before the meeting with my mom could be arranged, I had an appointment with Dr. Stephens to get blood work done. She said that everything looked really good and we could get started on testosterone. She also suggested that I see another doctor who specialized in male endocrinology, but he didn't have an opening until March 20. During the appointment, I asked her why she had asked to have the meeting with my mother, Sari, and me. She explained that my mom had asked her some questions and voiced some concern about my transition, and she thought it would be helpful if we all got together. But so far my mom hadn't agreed to a meeting time.

After I got the green light from Dr. Stephens, I tried to reach my mom and let her know that I was starting my transition on March 20. When she didn't return my call, I ended up sending her a text message with the news.

Again, I didn't hear anything back.

I had no proof that my mom was no longer comfortable with

me transitioning; it was just a feeling that something had shifted for her. It could have just been that she was busy working, but I knew in my gut that Mom was avoiding me and the reality of my impending transition. I understood implicitly that it's one thing to abstractly discuss the idea of a transition, and quite another to imagine the reality of your forty-year-old daughter suddenly becoming your son.

In February, I went to Palm Springs for my sister Chianna's eighteenth birthday. I had already told my brother Chez my news but had not had a chance to share it with Chianna or with my stepmother, Mary. When my sister invited Jenny and me down for her birthday, I thought it would be a good time to tell her what was going on.

Once in Palm Springs, I first approached Mary and told her about my plan. She asked me some health questions. And then she said, "If this is what you need to do to make you happy, then I totally support it and support you."

She then asked me if I would be comfortable telling her new husband, Connie Mack, a Republican congressman from Florida. I was, and he was totally cool about it. This was one of the first times I actually got to know him and I was thrilled it went so well.

Then I told my sister, who was the most supportive of all. Not only did the news not faze her in the least, but she also seemed genuinely happy for me. I barely had to even explain myself—she got it right away and it made perfect sense to her. I was so used to pleading my case, as if I had to tell my whole story in order for the listener to not think I was crazy, but that was completely unnecessary for Chianna.

"I think it's great," she said.

I was blown away. She really did think it was great.

All in all it was an amazing lesson that I should never judge a book by its cover. Here was the Republican side of the family being completely accepting, embracing, and supportive, and I say that as a lifelong active Democrat. I'm not trying to make a political statement, and I certainly don't mean to offend anyone; my point is that those of us who are politically active often demonize individuals of the opposing party instead of understanding that we are all just people.

Granted, Mary is not my mother; and everybody on that side of the family is a lot younger—Mary is in her late forties, Chez and Chianna were eighteen and twenty-one at the time, Connie was in his early forties—and their comfort with the idea of my transitioning may have been that the concept was more familiar to them than it was for my mom's family, who are from another generation. I also didn't grow up in that family, and perhaps that bit of distance made it easier for them to accept me.

In many ways, this experience of telling my family in Palm Springs was a turning point in my relationship with them in general—all for the better. For the next few months, I would go out and visit with them frequently. I realized that I really wanted to nurture my relationships with that side of the family in a regular way. I hadn't grown up in a family-centered family; my father barely had any contact with his own extended family; I didn't know his sisters, his father, or his mother. I spent a lot more time with my mom's family, but there were always times when my mom wouldn't speak to her mother; my mom and my aunt were close, but other than that, I didn't have a lot of context for the idea of cherishing your family. I really was beginning to understand that relationships are something you always have to work at and that you get out of relationships what you put into them. I was always clear about this with my girlfriends, but not as much with my friends and my family.

On the other hand, I couldn't get my mom on the phone, or my aunt on the phone, and in the one conversation I had with Elijah, he'd made it clear that my transitioning was making him really uncomfortable. He didn't say anything to me that was directly negative, but he was asking me so many questions about why I was doing it that I began to feel like I was on the witness stand.

Then suddenly it was March. This was a big month for me: I turned forty, I was five years sober, and I had an appointment to begin taking male hormones—all within a few weeks of one another.

On March 20, I drove myself to the doctor's office. Dr. Stephens was there, as was Dr. Clark, the male endocrinology specialist, who talked to me about what to expect, most of which I already knew. He asked me to tell him my story—why I wanted to transition and so on. By this point, hearing my own story felt anticlimactic to me. I felt only confident that what I was doing was right.

The doctor took more blood that day and then gave me a basic checkup. I left with a prescription for AndroGel.

I drove straight to the pharmacy, got the prescription filled, and went home. I started taking 1.25 g of AndroGel topically that day.

After all the years of fear, ambivalence, doubts, and emotional torture, the day had finally come. I was on testosterone, and I have never looked back—not once.

In April, I finally had that meeting with my mom, Dr. Stephens, and Sari. My body had not started changing—nothing was at all visible. I had been on the hormones for two or three weeks. The meeting was at Sari's office.

In the meeting, my mom said she was shocked that I had already started, and she had never received my text. She was very afraid of the way the press would handle my transition, of her career being negatively impacted by my actions, and how her friends would react.

The doctors were trying to answer her questions and address her fears, but she was clearly upset and having a very hard time with this new reality.

It was not a good meeting.

Then a few days later, she called me to tell me how bad she felt in the meeting, and that she thought Dr. Stephens had mis-led her into thinking that I wasn't going to start to transition for a long time. It then became clear that her take-away from her July conversation with Stephens was that I had a lot of weight to lose and so on before starting to transition. I think, in her mind, she had years before she would have to deal with it. Maybe she thought I wasn't actually going to go through with it. Years ago I had told her that I was going to transition after I got out of rehab and then had chickened out.

At one point on the phone that day, my mom asked me, "What do you want to be, a professional transgender person?"

I said, "If you're referring to the activist work that I used to do in the gay and lesbian community, then yes."

I have read many memoirs by transgender people who

transitioned before me, as a way to gain the understanding and courage to eventually transition myself. I can't express how much the encouraging words of Jenny Boylan, Jamison Green, and Matt Kailey helped me move out of the darkness of fear and indecision and into the light of self-acceptance. I desperately wanted to be able to give back to my community in the same way. I knew there were other people out there struggling in the same way that I had been for so many years, and I wanted to help them.

"This isn't the same thing," my mom said. "People don't want to hear about your transition, Chas. You'll be the butt of every joke on late-night television."

She also didn't understand why I'd hired a publicist and why I needed to discuss my transition publicly at all.

This is where my mom and I differed in opinion a lot. I knew intuitively that when I finally did come out as transgender, it was going to be a big press event. I knew I couldn't transition privately; I had already learned that lesson. If I'd thought I could have transitioned without the public finding out, I would have done it years before. So I wanted to handle the public nature of my transition in the best possible way, and that meant embracing it.

But my mom didn't get this. She was angry, hurt, and scared. She just wanted me to make a statement to the press and let it go. But I knew that handling it vaguely would only trigger the paparazzi and the tabloids: they would make up their own story. I knew I had to talk about the truth and make it *my* story. I also knew I wanted to write a book about my experience.

My mom was having a lot of trouble understanding my point

of view during what turned out to be an hour-long conversation that day.

But I was so comfortable with my transition by then that I didn't care if what she said turned out to be true. I didn't believe it would happen that negatively, but either way, I was no longer afraid. I had complete faith not only that was this the right thing for me to do personally, but that transitioning was an essential part of my journey on this planet. I knew no matter what happened I would be okay, and I would be taken care of. My mom had to find her own path on this journey.

Once I was on the hormones for a while, I started to feel really good. I had more energy, more focus, and I was less afraid of making changes. It was as if I had been depressed and suddenly an antidepressant kicked in—everything in my life seemed easier. I felt motivated to move forward in all ways. It felt like my body had finally gotten something that it really needed to function. One of the biggest ways this new focus impacted me was that I decided to go back to school and finish my bachelor's degree. It had always bothered me that I had never finished college—especially since I started working in the GLBT community in nineties. Everyone I worked with then seemed to have a college degree, except for me. I also thought an advanced education would provide me with a good backup plan for my life. I hadn't been successful in a career in a long time; I knew I was going to write another book, but that wasn't a career. I had to take care of myself—and school would lead me to either getting a degree so that I could become a therapist and work with young trans people, helping them with their process, or a master's in GLBT studies so that I could perhaps become a professor.

So I applied to Antioch College and was accepted. I started classes that summer. I don't think I could have done this if I hadn't transitioned.

From the moment I began taking testosterone, I felt different in my body. I felt stronger, more energetic, and my libido became intense. After about a month, I also noticed muscle growth and a redistribution of fat—my body looked different in the mirror. And even though I had never accentuated my body's female curves, the outline and shape of my body was changing. Another early change was noticeable hair growth. The hair on my legs became thicker and slightly darker; at about three months, hair around my navel began to grow and spread (by a year, this hair will have slowly grown to my chest) and I had a downy kind of blond peach fuzz on my face. When I was working out, I felt an increase in physical strength and was able to lift more weight with more ease. The only negative physical side effect that I experienced from the testosterone was acne, both on my face and upper body (my chest, shoulders, and back). I didn't have many breakouts my first time through puberty, but this time has been different; like most transitioning FTMs I have suffered from moderate to bad acne, which in your forties can feel quite embarrassing. Thank god for Proactiv Solution, or it would have been much worse. The other slightly embarrassing side effect I've had is a propensity for perspiration, especially in situations where I am even the slightest bit nervous.

Another noteworthy change was how I experienced my sexuality. Whereas before, as a woman, I would describe my sex drive as low to normal, it was now incredibly strong. It felt just the way men's sexual desire has always been described—like a physical need—and my sexual relationship with Jenny became better than ever because of this new intensity.

But the single most significant change was how incredibly happy I felt. Every part of me felt liberated. I was starting to feel comfortable in my body for the first time in my life. Confidence streamed through me. The more male I looked, the more male I felt, the more joyous I became.

My goal was to try and get through the first few months of my transition privately, so I could begin to get used to the effects of the testosterone, without the media breathing down my neck. I had shared the news with my closest friends and my family, but no one beyond that circle had become aware of what was happening to me, to my body.

Then my voice started to drop.

The publicist I had hired, Howard Bragman, who is known for helping public figures come out of the closet, had been talking to a couple of different news shows—*Dateline* and *20/20*—as well as *People* magazine about my story; we thought that I'd break my news in that kind of setting and then write a book. We also had a meeting with a producer who was interested in doing some kind of television show that documented the transition. He specialized in documentaries about real-life stories.

But nothing was coming together.

Then TMZ got hold of the story, and Howard came to an agreement with them on how to break it using a statement he would write. Jenny and I were in Palm Springs for Chianna's high school graduation when we got the news of this. We sent the statement to my mom's publicist so they were in the loop, too.

We were expecting it to break on a Monday, five days away. But then Howard called that following Thursday, three days later.

I was at home, with a new friend, Angie, whom I'd met in recovery and to whom I was trying to lend my support as she went through a breakup. Since getting sober, this was what made me feel most grounded in myself—giving back.

I was biding my time until my closest and oldest friend, Shula, came over with her baby Anabelle, my goddaughter, to spend the afternoon in our pool. I love kids and am especially close to Shula's baby. Anabelle is the only person who has known me only as a man.

Then Howard called me.

"The *National Enquirer*, has the story, and in order to beat them, TMZ has to go out with what we have right away."

"What's right away?" I asked.

"In half an hour," he said quickly.

"Shit," I said and hung up. I could feel the adrenaline build in my body.

Angie was getting ready to leave, and I realized that I had not even told her about my transitioning. I quickly tumbled out my story.

She was a bit surprised. "Wow—that's huge."

Then Shula arrived with Anabelle and instead of relaxing by the pool, I shuttled us to the cottage in the back of my house, away from the street.

I called Jenny, who was now in grad school getting her master's in education, to tell her that the story was about to break.

She said she was going to come home as soon as she could.

I sat frozen, feeling all of my life flashing before me: forty years of being in the press; being the focus of media attention because I had been on TV with my parents as a little kid; being outed as a lesbian, and now coming out again. After years of speculating as to what would happen if people knew I was transgender, I was finally going to find out. I felt relieved.

I'd wanted to do it this way. I'd learned the hard way how to deal with the press. I wasn't going to hide. But still, I was a bit trepidatious about how it was all going to unfold.

Twenty years ago that unfolding would have taken a few days, a week maybe, when stories were leaked to gossip columnists, then the tabloids, eventually finding their way onto the supermarket shelves. Now the Internet could explode a story within minutes, seconds even: your life, your privacy, splintered for millions of people to see all at once.

I called my mom, so she knew what was happening. I had barely talked to her since our last big conversation in April.

As always, she was calm in a crisis. She was supportive and kind and didn't seem fearful at all.

"Does Grandma know?" I asked her.

She told me that she and my aunt had just told my grandmother the weekend before at an impromptu birthday party. She said to me, "Grandma knows and she is fine."

It was a short but positive conversation. I was relieved. My mom was pulling through for me again.

I didn't know if the media was going to come to my house and knock on the door, or if they'd just gather in front, waiting for photo ops.

Then I started getting messages and random calls from people. Bruce Vilanch (the very successful comedy writer of *Hairspray* and the Oscars, and for Bette Midler and Whoopi Goldberg, and my fellow contestant from *Celebrity Fit Club*) left me a sweet message—he was really funny, very supportive. Then the comic Ant called me (he had been the host of *Celebrity Fit Club*), and then Larry King called me. All their voice mails were supportive and amazing: So far so good.

I decided to go online and check out the HRC and GLAAD Web sites. Thankfully, they had also posted really supportive statements. I hadn't known how the gay community was going to react. Of the few gay men I had already told, all had been supportive; but I didn't know what lesbians were going to say. I was ready with my response: "If you have a problem, I'm sorry."

But everyone was saying, "You're so brave to do this"—and other kinds of positive messages—just the opposite of my fears.

But I was still afraid to turn on the television.

Soon Jenny got home; she said no one was outside the house yet.

Shula left, and I kept getting random calls all day from people I knew—people I hadn't talked to in a while, and others who knew what was coming—and all their sentiments were very positive. I was so happy.

When I finally decided to turn on the TV, I figured CNN and MSNBC were safe, and to my shock and amazement, what I saw as breaking news in the crawl at the bottom of the TV screen was: "Sonny and Cher's Daughter Transitioning to Male."

"This is insane," I shouted. I couldn't believe that I was such big news.

I had a vague idea that things were going well, but over the next couple of days the tabloids came and started standing outside my house.

Then Jenny and I started getting followed, which was kind of ridiculous because I wasn't really doing anything interesting. The paparazzi would follow us to couples therapy, when I'd go to get a massage, go to the supermarket.

Some days there were about ten photographers on our block. It was annoying. But luckily their interest started to taper off.

CNN and Larry King had done pieces on transgender people, but I hadn't ever appeared. I knew that local trans activists were getting called to talk about me, and it seemed like I was at the point where I needed to start talking for myself. If I didn't, I was afraid that the media would take the story into their own hands and spin any small detail into anything they wanted.

And then Michael Jackson died.

In a millisecond all the attention shifted, and I was back again in my own life, in the midst of what I'd begun: my transition.

CHAPTER THIRTEEN

Out Again

Now that I was finally out as transgender man, I was anxious to be in touch with other trans guys. Except for talking with Davis in a therapeutic setting, I hadn't spoken to a single transgender man since that first conversation with Masen, all those years ago. Even though I had read many books about transitioning from female to male, I'd never had the opportunity to share my experience about the physical changes with anyone who had gone through the same process. I longed to have trans male friends that I could call up and ask all the questions in my head: How much longer was my voice going to keep cracking? When would I be able to grow a beard? A lot of guys reach out to FTM support groups while they are transitioning, but because of who I am and my desire for privacy, I didn't feel this was an option for me.

My publicist, Howard, put me in touch with Nick Adams, a gay transgender man who works for GLAAD. Just talking to Nick on the phone felt good. We hadn't even met in person, but I immediately felt comfortable, and he gave me an instant sense of the camaraderie and kinship that I love so much. Nick, who has become one of my good friends, also helped me get back in touch with Masen and set up a small gathering of trans men at my house.

A couple of weeks later, we were all together in my living room. Nick, Masen, Jake Finney, who works at the LA Gay & Lesbian Center and has since become a good friend, and Matthew, who works for the Transgender Law Center in San Francisco, all trans guys, were there for dinner. It was so great to see Masen again after so many years. He now seemed older and wiser, but with a familiar twinkle in his eyes when he smiled. Reconnecting with him made me feel like I had come full circle, and it really put my journey to becoming my true self into perspective. I was overjoyed to be out and in a room full of guys just like me.

Not surprisingly, I had a lot of questions for the group. Most trans guys seem to be obsessed with facial and body hair. I had just started to shave the copious amount of peach fuzz that was growing on my face. Nick told me to shave with a one or two-blade razor to avoid getting too close a shave that could lead to ingrown hairs. I also got the disappointing news that it could take up to two years before I started to grow coarser, beardlike facial hair, and anywhere from five to ten years to be able to grow a full, thick beard.

We talked about what these men remembered from the first stages of transitioning, how their families and spouses dealt with the process. We shared some thoughts on trans politics, as each of these men work in the "community." I was also curious about what they thought of how the media was covering the news of my transition. In general, they were all happy about the way the media was handling the situation and my story.

Then we got around to the specific experience they'd each had on hormones. I was only taking testosterone topically, not as injections, and I felt impatient with the physical results. I felt my male characteristics were unfolding too slowly and too subtly. Most of the guys shared that they'd used injectables for the first few years of their transition and believed that they got faster results. My topical dosage of AndroGel had been costing me about a hundred dollars per week, and insurance didn't cover it. When I learned from these other FTMs that most of them had started with testosterone in the form of injectables, and that it would cost me only about twenty dollars per month instead of a hundred dollars per week, I asked my doctors to switch. But they were reluctant, preferring that I move through the process more slowly. Eventually, I reached out to Dr. Horowitz, a doctor who treats a lot of the transgender people in Los Angeles.

Because treating transgender people with cross-hormone therapy (hormones of the opposite sex that change you from one gender to the other) is still relatively new, there have been no scientific studies that determine the long-term effects of this form of treatment. So instead of scientific data, you have schools of thought and doctors' opinions. I've spoken with a lot of different doctors about what form of testosterone is easiest on the body, topical or injectable, and I've received different opinions from all of them. So, under my doctor's care, and while being regularly monitored, I chose, for now, to use the injectable form of testosterone.

I was much happier with the results I was getting, and the money I was saving, by switching to injectable testosterone. My lower legs became much hairier—even my butt became hairier, which was one area that Jenny noticed before I did. My acne increased, and the tissue of my breasts began to break down and they started to drop.

But it's important to point out that everyone going through this process reacts differently, and there are many variations on how FTMs respond to hormones and how soon or intensely the male characteristics appear. Your genetic background is going to impact how you respond to testosterone. I am half Sicilian and a quarter Armenian—I expected to be hairy. But so far, that's not the case. I have always had fine hair and not much of it, and that probably is not going to change all that much—even when my hair begins to grow in more densely. The texture of my hair might get a little coarser, but probably I will never be as hirsute as some other trans guys. Some FTMs, for example, can never grow a beard; others seem to be able to grow facial hair within a few months of taking testosterone; and still for others it can take up to ten years on hormones. The same is true of losing your hair. If you are genetically predisposed to male pattern baldness, you will begin to lose your hair once you start on hormones. Since this doesn't run in either side of my family, I am pretty confident about keeping what I've got on top.

So over the course of the summer, my body hair grew thicker, my voice continued to deepen, and my overall physique became ever more male; my body was still changing. My beard seemed like it was growing in, and the hair felt more like whiskers. I was thrilled. Then when I went into the bathroom to look more closely, I realized that the hair was growing only on one side of my face. As soon as Jenny came home, she confirmed my lopsided beard!

Overall I felt an enormous sense of empowerment. I had returned to college to finish my undergraduate degree, and I was formulating ways in which I wanted to become politically active for the trans community—perhaps not in the same way as I had for the GLBT community, but in a more therapeutic way. Jenny was taking the journey with me, and we were handling the twists and turns very well. My life was finally falling into place—with the exception of my relationships with my aunt and my mom.

I have always been very close to my aunt, my mother's sister, and I had been trying to talk with Gee ever since I knew I was going to start my transition. She knew that I had begun the transition process, but we had not really spoken about it. I kept trying to reach her, but it felt like she was avoiding the conversation. She was traveling; she was sick; she was getting back from traveling. She would text me and say, "I am sorry, I know I'm supposed to call you. . . ."

I eventually got annoyed. At first, I felt that if Gee didn't want to deal with me, that was her prerogative and I would just let it go. Then the older, wiser part of me knew that I really loved this person and I needed to keep trying to reach out. With testosterone in my system now, it's much easier for me to be more defensive and stubborn when my feelings get hurt, so I really had to force myself to keep pursuing communication.

I finally got Gee on the phone and she admitted that she was having a hard time with my transition, which I already suspected. I had tried to talk with Gee years ago when I first started to suspect that I might be transgender. At that time my aunt told me that she thought I was wrong and that I must be confusing some other issue I was having with the need to become male. It was disappointing to me that Gee was so adamantly opposed to the idea that I might be transgender then, and as everyone on that side of the family has a bit of a stubborn streak, we hadn't really broached the subject again.

As Gee and I talked and she shared her thoughts and feelings about me transitioning now, I tried to be as empathetic as I could, telling her, "I get it—it's weird, it's strange, it's hard—it's not the norm—it's all of those things." I tried to put myself in my aunt's frame of mind as to how jarring it must be to know me one way for forty years and then have to get used to something totally different. We talked about a lot of different issues, and I tried to explain to her that this is who I have always been and that I couldn't go on living a life that was essentially a lie.

Slowly our conversation shifted, from my transition to the topics that we have always talked about. My aunt and I have always been very similar, appreciating a simpler life, out of the limelight. By the end of the conversation Gee said, "You're the same," and I said, "I know I'm the same." It's that fear of the unknown that often keeps people apart.

This wasn't the case with my mom.

At the end of June, I got a long text from my mom. In it she said that she had called me and gotten my new outgoing message, hearing for the first time how my voice had dropped. She said in her text that hearing the change in my voice devastated her. The reality of my transition had finally hit her. Then she explained that she was having a really hard time and that she couldn't see or talk to me for the time being.

In some ways, I was relieved by this text. I had been feeling that she was having a hard time dealing with my transition but that she wouldn't say anything about how she was feeling.

Now I knew. I also felt that now that she was beginning to express her feelings, a more complete healing process could begin.

On the other hand, I was hurt that she didn't want to have any contact with me. I knew that this was not her rejecting me, and I understood that this was her process, but I couldn't help but feel a little abandoned, especially after we had become so close again. I decided to take this request as a need to grieve the loss of her daughter.

During the summer, as I ventured out in public in a more regular way, returning to my life, as it were, I began to notice that people were reacting to me differently. On a couple of occasions, they seemed to hesitate before addressing me, as if they were trying to figure out whether to refer to me as a "sir" or a "ma'am." I was going through the androgynous phase of the transition. I didn't look decisively male or female. I still had breasts, but I was binding them down so that they would be less obvious. My upper body was starting to become more muscular, and my face was starting to look a bit more hardened, but it hadn't yet lost all of its female characteristics. It was an odd, but exhilarating, time.

Meanwhile, my publicist received some calls from people interested in doing a documentary about my transition. I had never thought of doing a documentary film about my transition, but I really liked the idea of it. Transitioning is such a visual process that it made perfect sense to me to capture it on film and give a whole new audience a chance to understand what the process entails. We took several meetings with different directors and production companies before I decided to do a documentary with the production company World of Wonder, because I had really liked some of their other films—*The Eyes of Tammy Faye* and *Monica in Black and White* for example. They had also done a short series, *TransGeneration*, profiling four trans college students. I truly felt World of Wonder had the best understanding of the issues around being transgender. Randy Barbato and Fenton Bailey, the owners of WOW, began to film Jenny and me in September of 2009 and continued for eighteen months. Having grown up in front of a camera, I don't find the process of filming a documentary that difficult. There have definitely been times when I would have rather not had a camera following me around, but that's mostly because I see how it makes other people feel uncomfortable. Ever since I worked for GLAAD, I have understood the power of media to open hearts and minds about GLBT issues, and this was my number-one motivation for wanting to document my transition on film and tell the full scope of my story in this book.

Also that summer, I was finally able to afford top surgery. I had gotten the deal for this book but hadn't yet been paid, so I temporarily borrowed the money from my sponsor Jane. I booked the procedure for September 23, when I knew I'd have a break from school. My breasts, which had long been a burden and a sign of my female biology, were finally going to be gone.

I had been researching surgeons for a while and made the decision to have Dr. Michael L. Brownstein in San Francisco do the surgery. I had sent him photos of my breasts, and I now had to get some blood work done and have a regular preoperational physical. Obviously, I was a bit worried about the painkillers that would be involved. Since I have a fairly low pain tolerance, I knew I would need to take some pain medication, which would automatically start the phenomenon of craving again. And once under the influence of pain meds, I am incapable of making decisions about them. So I made arrangements for someone to hold my medication and to dole it out to me only as prescribed by my doctor.

In the week or so before the surgery, as I was getting ready for it, World of Wonder's Fenton and Randy started shooting the documentary. Jenny had finished her first year of graduate school at the end of the summer. In preparation for my top surgery, it was strongly suggested that I quit smoking cigarettes, something I had been doing since I was sixteen years old. I have to admit that I absolutely loved to smoke, and I truly believed that I wouldn't enjoy my life as much as a nonsmoker. But I quit cold turkey, without the use of any form of nicotine replacement, by reading the book *The Easy Way to Stop Smoking* by Allen Carr. (I have now been a nonsmoker for over a year and know that I'll never go back. I would highly recommend this book to anyone who wants to quit smoking. I am so grateful to be rid of that last, and in some ways, most insidious addiction.)

There are two different kinds of procedures for the construction of a male chest from a female chest. The keyhole method, which is only suitable for patients with little breast tissue, consists of making a small incision around part of the areola and removing the breast tissue through that incision. Because of my large breasts, I wasn't a candidate for this procedure. My surgery is known as the double incision method with nipple graft. In this procedure the surgeon removes all the breast tissue and skin and then, using your original nipples, constructs male-size areolas and nipples, and replaces them in the proper position for a male chest. This surgery leaves two large scars underlining the pec muscles, and faint scars around the areolas.

Jenny and I, along with the film crew, left for San Francisco, where my surgery was going to take place, the day before. We met with my surgeon so he could examine me and explain the details prior to my procedure, scheduled for first thing in the morning. After this meeting I felt very assured and confident about my surgery.

I had texted my mom with the date that I was having top surgery, and she called me the day before my operation. She was calm and said, "Don't be nervous, it will be fine." It was a quick conversation, but again it felt reassuring to talk to her, even though I hadn't spoken to her for a while. I was just glad that she called me.

Jenny and I arrived at the hospital at six in the morning so I could be checked in and prepped for procedure. I was excited that after so many years of waiting I would soon have the chest I'd always wanted. But I was also feeling a little nervous about the surgery going smoothly, and whether or not I would feel really weak or in a great deal of pain afterward. As they wheeled me into the operating room, I kissed Jenny and told her that I loved her and would see her soon.

When I woke up, I was in less pain than I'd thought I was going to be. The pain medicine worked just fine; I was comfortable, and I felt really happy that it was over.

Jenny called my family and close friends to tell them that all had gone well. I remember that I talked to my mom, though not much of the conversation. I was pretty out of it for most of that first day in the hospital, but by that night I was starting to feel more lucid. I checked out of the hospital first thing the next morning and was taken to my friend Lisa's house in Sausalito to recover. I ended up staying in the Bay Area for a week.

At first, I had drains coming out of my chest to collect excess fluid, which needed to be emptied every few hours. I had to write down how much fluid was draining. I also had a massive bandage covered by a compression binder to keep fluid from collecting in my chest—since the body wants to fill the area where the breasts used to be with fluid, which causes swelling and slows down the healing process. After five days, I went to see my doctor for my first follow-up visit. He took the drains out. It felt very odd—one side hurt; one side didn't.

He also took off a special kind of bandage I had been wearing that was connected to the nipple grafts. When that came off, I got to see my new chest for the first time. It nearly took my breath away. My breasts were finally gone. I felt relieved and overjoyed. The doctor put on a light bandage, and then two days after that, he took out my stitches.

Soon after, Jenny and I flew home to LA. Since I couldn't lift anything heavy, I had to ask for help to get my bag off the luggage carousel. But that was the worst of it.

I do admit to feeling weird for a while. I wasn't in pain after a week or so, but my chest felt really tight and numb where the incisions had been made. I could take the binder off in the shower—and that part of my body just felt strange, and very sensitive. Even the water from the shower felt intense. But it was all worth it.

In the weeks and months following my top surgery, I looked in the mirror and saw a man. This was truly an amazing feeling.

The first time I took off my shirt without cringing was simply stunning—something I hadn't felt since puberty set in some thirty years ago. As life-altering as I'd imagined having top surgery would be, I'd underestimated the scope of the impact that it would have on the way I now looked and felt. My new chest made me feel completely free and completely male. Now I rarely wear a shirt when I am at home.

Soon after my top surgery, I began to speak out in the media. I knew that after this procedure, news about my transition would start circulating again, and it was my natural instinct to talk to reporters, in the hope of helping others in the trans community. I appeared on *Entertainment Tonight* and *Good Morning America*. I wanted to put a positive spin on my transition and wanted to take control of the way the media covered my top surgery. In interviews I tried to stick only to the topic of my top surgery, and speak to the issues for the trans community, and for the most part, everything went according to that plan. The one question that did make me a bit uncomfortable was whether or not I was planning on having sexual reassignment, or bottom surgery. In truth, most of us trans people seem to be much less concerned about what we have between our legs than everyone else seems to be. The vast majority of FTMs never have bottom surgery. It's very expensive, not covered by health insurance, and the results are still not very good. For now, I've decided to keep my privates private.

In spite of some uncomfortable questions, I like doing interviews. I'm good on my feet. I always look at these media appearances as a way to reach people, and now I wanted to educate others about trans issues and broaden people's minds about what being transgender is all about. I also wanted to speak to how painful it can be not to transition and explain why I wanted to go through this process and have top surgery. I believe that when anyone hears or watches a story about someone who is different in some way, they come away with a more expanded view of the world in general. To me, being a spokesperson is about opening people's hearts and minds and promoting tolerance.

Watching those interviews now, I realize I still looked very androgynous then, even though my breasts were gone. Over the next year, more subtle changes would start to occur, making me look more and more male. It's virtually impossible to pinpoint the exact structural changes that occur on one's face during transition. I would say that the closest approximation is putting one's facial features through a kind of strainer, where all soft feminine characteristics of your face are slowly sifted away.

During the summer of 2009, I met a six-year-old FTM child named EJ. His mom had posted a blog about her son, and on that Labor Day, I was invited over to meet Dawn and EJ.

At first EJ was a bit shy with me, even though he knew I was a trans man. He is an adorable little boy, who looks like a young Harry Potter. But he seemed kind of scared of me at first and was far more comfortable with Jenny. I let him have his space for a while, but when he was swimming in the pool, I jumped in and started roughhousing with him, launching onto the rafts and having races. Soon EJ felt much more at ease.

These kids have become really important to me. Since meeting EJ, I have become involved with a playgroup and support group for families of trans kids that Dawn started. Transforming Family meets one Sunday every month. There is also a support group for the parents run by a therapist, a playgroup for younger children, and a peer rap group for the adolescents that Nick Adams and I facilitate. In addition to our regular monthly gatherings, I've also taken a few of the young kids to Disneyland with Dawn and helped to organize an informational seminar for parents of trans kids from all over California. We invited Dr. Jo Olson from Children's Hospital to give a presentation on hormone blockers and treatment, and a lawyer from the Transgender Law Center, a California-based legal advocacy organization, came and spoke about the legal issues around name and gender change. Nick, Andrea James, an LA-based transgender activist, and I led a panel discussion on issues we face from an adult transgender perspective, and Kim Pearson of TransYouth Family Allies talked about work she does with schools and camps on behalf of transgender children and adolescents.

All of this outreach felt and feels enormously satisfying for me. In the fall of 2009, my old friend Masen asked me to go to San Francisco for the Transgender Law Center's yearly fund-raising event. I've done a million of such events for the gay community, and they always felt like work. Now I was able to approach these events in a much more positive light. This is simply because I am so much more myself now. I'm more social. I'm happy.

As I made my way around the room at the TLC fund-raiser, the fact that I was a gamer came up. Word quickly spread. Suddenly this pastime of mine (something that used to drive Jenny crazy because she felt I used video gaming as an escape) made so much sense to me. Many of us at this party loved playing video games because they allowed us to choose the sex of our character, the way our characters looked and dressed. I discovered that the trans community is filled with nerds—fantasy-loving, *Star Wars/Harry Potter/Lord of the Rings*—obsessed individuals, including myself. Video games are filled with odd people triumphing over evil. It all fits perfectly. In the trans community, I had not only found my peers in an emotional sense, I had found my cultural home, too. This event gave me my first real sense of belonging to that community.

About three weeks after my top surgery, Jenny's family had a reunion in Las Vegas. This was going to be the first time I would be seeing Jenny's parents and the rest of her clan since I had begun transitioning.

We were staying at a hotel, where the service staff consistently addressed me as "sir." Before surgery, when I looked more androgynous, I would get called "sir" sometimes, other times "ma'am." From the moment I had my top surgery, there was no longer any hesitation: I was a sir, just like I'd always wanted to be.

One of the goals that I was striving for by transitioning was for people to relate to me as the man that I had always felt I was on the inside. I never really thought about it in terms of passing or not passing; I just really wanted my physical appearance to match how I felt internally. So when people address me as "sir," they are acknowledging my true identity—the real me. I know that this is not important to everybody who transitions, and I'm not saying it should be every transgender person's goal, just that for me, finally being treated like a man feels good and right.

I was also happy to not have to kiss or hug a man hello as I always did as a woman. Now I could simply put out my hand to shake. The first time Aunt Gee and Uncle Ebar came over to say hello, I went to give my uncle a hug, and he said, "Straight guys don't hug each other," and stuck out his hand. I was grateful for the etiquette lesson.

Later in the fall, I was traveling to an event, and when I got off the plane, I really had to go to the bathroom. I couldn't wait until I got to my hotel. Up to that point, I had avoided this situation by always waiting until I got home or to a private place. But this time that wasn't possible. So I kept my hat low and head down as I entered the men's room for the first time. There was a long line, and since I had to wait for a stall, I turned to the guy behind me to say "I am waiting for a stall" when a urinal opened up. It was awkward the first time, but now I've gotten over it. Unlike in the ladies' room, men don't socialize with one another in public restrooms. Some other trans guys told me to just go in and take care of my business, and not talk to other guys unless absolutely necessary.

Other than those two instances, male behavior has been very easy for me to adapt to. People who aren't transgender might believe that learning to behave as the opposite gender would be incredibly difficult, but for me trying to behave like a woman was the real challenge. I didn't really have to learn how to act like a man because in my head I'd always been one. I already knew how a man stands, dresses, combs his hair, and hails a cab. I was born with this knowledge, and as soon as I stopped trying to pass as a woman, I knew how to live as a man.

As the year was winding down, I was starting to feel at home in my new physical body, which after more than forty years was amazing. All of my life seemed to be settling into place, and I felt very positive about what the new year had to offer, including a hope to truly reconnect with my mom before too much more time passed.

Jenny and I were both craving a relaxing, stress-free Christmas and were planning on spending it in Palm Springs with my stepmom Mary, her husband Connie, Chez, and Chianna. Mary always made everything beautiful for Christmas—the tree, the house, delicious food. That year was no different. On Christmas we all exchanged gifts and spent a wonderful day and evening hanging out, playing board games, and eating a great dinner. It was totally mellow, with no drama. As an ending to an eventful year, the calm ordinariness of that holiday felt like a perfect cap.

Ever since transitioning, I hear all the time that I seem so grounded, so present, so happy. And I am. This recognition of how comfortable I now am in my own skin means a lot to me and is further affirmation that I made the right choice, despite how hard it was. It also underscores not only how uncomfortable I used to feel in my old body, but also the way that physical discomfort must have played out in my behavior and sense of confidence. In retrospect, I think I might have given off signals for people to keep their distance from me. As if protecting myself from feeling even more ill at ease, I didn't want people to get too close to me. For decades I knew I didn't make sense as a girl— not just to myself but to others around me. It was impossible for me to really be myself in front of other people, at first because I didn't know who I was, and later because I thought I would be rejected by anyone who really knew my secret.

My sister Chianna has said to me, "After your transition, it was so much easier for me to relate to you." She said that "when I viewed you as a girl, I thought, you are such a different kind of girl than me. We just had nothing in common." She told me that she hadn't known how to relate to me. But since I transitioned, it's become clear to her that I am "just a guy," and that makes much more sense to her. Now we are really close, we talk regularly and see each other often. I am now her big brother and give her advice from a male perspective, a way of connecting that makes perfect sense to both of us. I have always had a typically male relationship with my brother Chez, and in some ways, we've been very similar; we have the same kind of temperament, have similar tastes in movies and books, and share a love of history, conspiracy theories, and gaming. He was the first person on my dad's side of the family that I told about my transition, and he was cool with it right away. My brother Elijah didn't feel totally comfortable when I first told him I was transitioning. He wasn't unsupportive, but I think he didn't fully understand why I would want to change my gender, and he felt scared about me changing or feeling different toward him in some way. Since I transitioned, Elijah has been very supportive and even told me, "I thought your transition was going to be a really big deal, but when I spend time with you now, I realize that this is the person that you've always been."

I can see this improvement in most of my close relationships—with Uncle Ebar and Aunt Gee, Jenny's parents, my friends, as well as my brother Elijah. One friend of mine told me he never knew how to relate to me because my gender was off. He said, "I never knew how to greet you; it always seemed weird to give you a kiss hello. Now I get you; you're a guy, and I just shake your hand." I make more sense to him now, too.

This is also true when I am out in the world. Before, I was perceived as a woman who was displaying extremely gender-variant behavior (wearing suits, men's clothing, and so on), and men and women both were standoffish. I also believe that my inner discomfort level was palpable to others and worked as an invisible repellent. I never realized this difficulty others had relating to me because I had nothing to compare it to. But since there is now alignment between my internal and external identity, this self-consciousness is gone. Now I am treated in a much friendlier manner, as a peer, in particular, by men.

One example comes to mind. The parking attendant at my therapist's office, who has ignored me for years, now says, "Hey, buddy, how's it going?" every time I arrive for my appointment. I experience something similar with every salesperson, every waiter, every valet—everywhere I go. People are a lot nicer to me now that I am definably male. There seems to be a bond or understanding that men have with one another that either doesn't exist between women or I was never privy to, because of my gender dysphoria. I can't express how good it feels to be shown kindness and acceptance by men that I don't even know.

In a more subtle way, my interaction with straight women has changed, too. Before my transition, I often found myself a bit uncomfortable around straight women whom I didn't know; now I feel more at ease. I've also noticed a hard-to-define sexual tension that seems to color all interactions between heterosexual men and women. I am not suggesting that all relationships between men and women are sexual in nature, but merely that on some kind of primal, biological level that tension always exists. At least that is how I now perceive it.

I also now realize what an extreme disadvantage gender-variant people have in our society. I never saw how much my gender incongruity put people off until it was gone. I never experienced outward hostility, but I was often just kind of ignored. The fact is that now that I look and act appropriately male, the world has become a much friendlier place. Though I am happy about my life now, I can't help but think it's horrible how certain segments of our society treat gender-variant individuals. It's time people understood that though there are primarily two biological sexes, there are numerous ways in which people express their own individual gender identity, all of which should be accepted.

CHAPTER FOURTEEN

Peace

Over the past year, as my transition has progressed, I've found myself reaching out to people from my past. I was inspired to do this by the actions of my mom, who recently reconnected with Paulette, an old friend of hers. Paulette had been part of our life since I was a child, but for some reason or other she and my mom lost touch.

When I heard from my aunt Gee that my mom and Paulette were back in touch, I was very excited. I couldn't wait to see her again. She had been my mom's assistant when I was a baby, and they had been best friends after that for over twenty-five years. But I hadn't seen her in fifteen years. In late winter, my brother Elijah had an art opening that Jenny and I attended, along with my mom and the rest of my family and close friends. At the opening, I looked around at a lot of people my family had known over the years. And then I saw Paulette. I walked over to Pauley and gave her a big hug. She was so happy to see me that she started crying. She wasn't in the least bit fazed that I had transitioned. I was deeply struck by the realization that all my life Paulette had known someone who was not really me, and now it felt amazing to share my real self with this person I had known and loved for so long.

Getting reconnected with Paulette was the trigger for me to reach out to many other people from my past. A lot of people had slipped away from my life while I was using drugs. I had pushed people way, withdrawn from my network for so long, and now I felt it was time to let my guard down. Some people asked me why I had stayed away, as if they might have done something. Of course it wasn't that. It was that keeping up with relationships wasn't something I could do before—I felt too mixed up, too disjointed within myself, too unhappy.

One of the people I reconnected with was Heidi, my ex-girl-friend and former bandmate. For me, it was really important to reestablish this connection as part of a larger healing process. I wanted her to see who I really was. I had buried so much of who I was when I was with her. First, I did so unconsciously, wanting to please her, make her love me—since that was my nature at the time. No request that she made was too much for me. Then later, as our music career got started, we both had to pretend we were something we weren't—that we weren't together, that we weren't lesbians. We made destabilizing compromises all the time.

To be honest, I was really nervous to reach out to Heidi. It had been almost a decade since we had spoken to each other. We had been through so much together, both positive and negative. But I took the leap. I initially contacted her through Facebook, and then before long we were e-mailing and talking on the phone.

When we met again in person, it was healing for both of us. We were both reminded of why we had been together in the first place—not in the romantic or sexual sense, but in the fact that we had a real connection. We got each other. We were talkers and banterers, and we fell right back into this. She ended up staying at my house until about one in the morning, and we were talking nonstop the entire time. It felt like reconnecting with a sibling. It was just a good thing all around.

Heidi didn't realize that I hadn't known that I was trans when I was with her—she felt relieved when I told her this because it meant that I hadn't kept it from her at the time. I had always interpreted her wanting to change me as criticism of me. At the time, she felt she was looked down upon for being so femme and consequently felt a lot of pressure when she was first coming out to dress and act in a certain way herself. She never felt comfortable in the box that she felt placed in by the older feminist-lesbians she knew. She enjoyed wearing makeup, shaving, and having her nails done. So by the time she met me, she thought she had found a new way to be a lesbian that worked for her—essentially a lipstick lesbian. So she thought she was liberating me to be my own kind of lesbian, too.

Reconnecting with people from my past has been a gift of transitioning that I would have never anticipated before starting this journey. In addition to Heidi, I have gotten back in touch with my best friend from childhood, Gina, and my close high school friend Orfeh. I also reconnected with Suzanne and Dori, whom I had met through Joan when I was still a teenager. As I started to really examine my life, I often thought about those two women I had so identified with as a child. I began to wonder if the reason I identified with them, more than any other lesbians I ever met, was perhaps because they weren't really lesbians after all. When I got together with Dori and Suzanne, who were still best friends, the three of us went out to dinner. Seeing them was really amazing, and after answering all of their questions about my transition, I asked them if they had ever thought about doing it. Both Suzanne and Dori told me that they had talked about transitioning many times, but that now that they were in their late fifties, they felt that it was too late for them to make such a change. But they believed that if they had been born into a later generation, they would have probably transitioned.

I can't really express in words how profound it is for me to finally let people from my past get to know and understand me for who I really am.

In the new year, one person in my life had continued to keep her distance—my mom. I hadn't seen my mother since the spring and hadn't had any contact since the conversations we had before and right after my top surgery. When I first received the long text she sent me explaining her need for some space, I tried to understand how difficult my transition must be for her. However, as time went on with no contact from her, I began to feel more rejected, hurt, and angry. For the first time in my life, I was feeling so good and whole, and now my mother wouldn't see me or talk to me. I felt sad that something that was making me feel so happy would make my mom feel so bad.

Of course, I could appreciate how difficult this radical change must be for her. In some ways the transition process is like a death, because part of you is gone forever. Whatever small part of me was female before I started this process was now truly gone. And I could understand that my mom was grieving the loss of the person she perceived her daughter to be. However, I was still very much alive, and missing her.

Then finally, in late January of 2010, my mom made contact

with me. She called and asked me and Jenny to come to dinner. She had started dating someone new, and I hadn't met him. This man had encouraged my mom to face her fear and see me. Elijah was there for part of the dinner, too. My mom's new boyfriend cooked. We hung out in the den and talked for a while. It was all very casual.

As independent and grown-up as I like to think I am, it felt really good to see my mother after so long. It had been ten months since the previous April, when we had had the therapy session. In some ways it felt like no time at all had gone by, as if nothing much had happened since the last time we saw each other. But obviously a lot had changed.

I didn't want to make my transition the main topic of discussion throughout the evening, and I didn't want to force my mother to discuss something she wasn't ready to deal with. I wanted to respect her process. It took almost ten years for me to come to terms with being transgender; it was going to take time for my mom to become comfortable with my transition, too. We stuck to talking about family, business, politics, films, and television—our usual safe topics. I felt the presence of a large pink elephant in the room all through the evening. This did make me a bit uncomfortable I have to admit, but I was trying to let my mom take the lead. I figured she would talk about my transition when she was ready.

The internal changes I experienced during the start of my transition feel pretty stable now; however, I have noticed some additional emotional shifts. I have a temper now, which I never had before starting testosterone. For the most part it's very easy to control, but occasionally I have to reel in my anger before I risk saying something hurtful. In general, I am more aggressive and experience emotions viscerally. Communication is also a bit different for me as well. I can't or don't like to talk as much as I used to. I find that women seem to have the ability to talk endlessly about things, recounting every little detail. I no longer have that ability. In fact when I'm around such chatter, it starts to drive me crazy. When I'm with a group of women, like at my sponsor's house for our monthly brunch and step group, I often hit a wall, where I just can't talk or listen to others talk anymore. I start to feel like I want to jump out of my skin and I have to get up and do something physical, such as clear everyone's dishes from the table. The most surprising emotional change that I've experienced is that my eyes really tear up now when something moves me. I have never been a crier before, but I have noticed that sometimes when I'm watching a movie or a show on TV that touches me, I get all choked up.

My outward physical changes continue, though very subtly. If you filmed someone transitioning over an eight-year period and then watched the whole thing sped up, it would probably look something like when a man transforms into a werewolf in the movies; however, the day-to-day reality is that these changes happen very slowly. For example, there is a thin bare patch in one of my sideburns that is less obvious now than it was three months ago. By the time this book is published, it will probably be gone altogether, and by then I may be able to grow something else on my face.

My face and head seem bigger and more square or rectangular now. I've lost the more petite, roundish quality my face used to have. More hair continues to grow, and more thickly, on my body and face. This is part of the gradual, evolving process of transforming into a male. I know my hands look more masculine. My skin is tougher. My veins are all more visible. All of this together makes me appear more male.

I have to remember that I am going through a second puberty. When I get impatient, I remind myself that boys don't change into men overnight. It takes years before they grow out of that awkward in-between stage. The same will be true for me. For most trans guys, this is a five- to seven-year period of change, which is far slower than I thought it would be at the outset of this process.

Changes that I am less aware of are also happening.

Jenny says I am now less sweet, as if my female essence is gone. She tells me sometimes that she feels like she is dating my twin brother. My friend and lawyer Dina recently watched the documentary film I made with World of Wonder Productions and cried. She said part of her really missed "the old, sweet Chaz." Though I don't miss the old me, watching the documentary, now titled *Becoming Chaz*, has made me more aware of just how much I've changed both physically and emotionally over the past eighteen months. Giving a film crew such intimate access to my life, and the life I share with Jenny, has given me the opportunity to observe myself, and my behavior. It's helped me to understand the transition that my loved ones have had to make in going through this process with me.

At first, I heard these kinds of remarks with disdain—how could they miss that part of me that I always associated with being uncomfortable, feeling depressed, and having no confidence? But gradually, I have begun to understand both what these people are missing and why I should acknowledge their feelings. I certainly don't miss that part of myself. I see myself as having been weak, vulnerable, and meek, and I'm not any of those things now. I don't think I am less sweet; I just think I am not passive anymore.

Some of these changes—subtle or not—are directly related to the testosterone. My increased sex drive and more aggressive nature are totally driven by that hormone in my body. But I think some of the changes, like feeling much more relaxed in social settings or when meeting new people, are simply the result of feeling comfortable in my body for the first time ever. I'm finally myself, body and soul. The ultimate cause or trigger for the change is not really that important to me. I simply feel good and like being this way.

But life still intervenes, no matter how happy I am now. After Christmas that year, Jenny and I started having a hard time. She started drinking and smoking pot. She seemed to be depressed.

Part of me knew she was regressing from all the stress of my transition, but neither of us were really dealing with the impact of it on our relationship. As we headed toward March, however, and the first-year anniversary of my transition, I began to feel like our lives were going in two different directions.

My views on alcohol or drug abuse are very clear. I don't drink or use drugs, and it is my hope that Jenny, as a self-described alcoholic, won't either, though I know I can't control what others do. But for some months I'd been watching her become progressively worse. She started out drinking nonalcoholic beer. That moved into drinking regular beer once a week. Soon she added pot. I didn't know the full extent of her using for quite a while, because she would wait until I had gone to bed to do it.

As a late bloomer, I feel a lot of pressure to make the most of what I'm doing now. Let's be honest—I "came to at thirty-five" with the skill set of a twenty-five-year-old. I had to work really hard to start to grow, and it's really important to me. I had to do so much work on myself, such as go to therapy, recovery meetings, do the steps, and finally transition, in order to feel good about myself. And then there was Jenny acting out in a lot of the ways that I had finally addressed in myself, although I must take into account that she is six and a half years younger than me.

To celebrate the one-year anniversary of my transition, I decided to give myself a big party, to commemorate the most important year of my life thus far. Jenny, who had worked as an event planner, and I had been planning and organizing the party for weeks. This was going to be the first time in my life that I had ever given myself a party, and it was going to be a huge event. Randy and Fenton were going to film it as part of the documentary. We had invited close to eighty people, including our most important friends and family—everyone in my life who had supported me through my transition.

The party was amazing. I felt thrilled to have so many people who loved and supported me gathered in one place.

But that night, after all of the guests and the film crew had left, Jenny got really drunk with a couple of her friends from school. I felt very resentful toward her.

At first I hadn't wanted to see how much her drinking had progressed, and I hadn't wanted to deal with my feelings around that. But slowly I became more and more upset by the fact that my thirty-four-year-old girlfriend stayed up drinking all night with guys from her class who were in their early twenties. The level of anger that I was feeling toward Jenny was something new to me. In the past when Jenny had relapsed, I had felt sad and scared, but now all I could feel was bitter anger and disappointment. This caused me to shut down, and I became very distant and cold toward her. I know the way that I was acting toward Jenny was very difficult for her and unproductive, but at the time I just couldn't let my anger go.

In the weeks that followed, Jenny realized that she had fallen far behind in her schoolwork, and figured out that in order to graduate she was going to have to spend the next three months basically locked in the library at UCLA. As is typical with her style of alcohol abuse, she stopped drinking deliberately and immediately and refocused her attention on trying to finish her dissertation.

I was happy she was now taking her graduation and dissertation seriously and felt better that she had stopped drinking and was focused on school, but I also felt a lingering resentment and distrust.

We were not spending any time together, but the underlying issues that we were both feeling were still there, with neither of us dealing with anything about our relationship.

When I now think about that time, I realize we were in very different places. We both just wanted for Jenny to graduate—both of us focused on that end goal in June. I knew things were not good between us, but I didn't want to bring up anything that would interfere with the work Jenny had to do. I tamped down my feelings about what had gone on in the previous months, knowing they would come to light eventually.

Literally the day after her graduation, everything exploded. We were hosting a brunch in Jenny's honor, and Jenny wanted to cancel it. In retrospect, this was probably because she was exhausted. We started to fight, and Jenny's temper exploded.

I was so angry I almost walked out.

We made it through the day, barely. Interestingly, most of this was caught on film and is in our documentary.

Over the next couple of months, things went from bad to worse. We tried harder in couples therapy, but at times even that safe haven was excruciating.

I became kind of obsessed with Jenny's behavior: I was focused on all the things about her that I wanted her to change.

One day after a recovery meeting for the family and friends of alcoholics, I went to lunch with some good friends of mine from this program. I was going on and on about the parts of Jenny's behavior that I didn't like, how I couldn't trust her since her relapse, and how I didn't know if our relationship was going to last. Then my friend Jason remarked that perhaps I was too focused on Jenny and that I needed to put the focus back on myself. This was just the kind of reframe I needed.

I then talked to another friend of mine—a trans guy in the program, who had also transitioned while in a relationship with the woman he has since married. She relapsed. This friend pointed out that by staying so focused on Jenny's behavior, I was losing sight of my own. He also pointed out that Jenny was entitled to her reaction—after all, her partner had undergone a sex change; it was no small event.

I suddenly heard Jenny in a different way. She had been saying to me for months, "You're different; you used to be sweet. You're not the same anymore." These comments had just made me angry. I hated the person she was missing—the sad, depressed, half person. My friend pointed out that I couldn't just invalidate Jenny's feelings.

"It's true, Chaz. You have changed. And our partners have real feelings about this."

This was my first adult sober relationship. In every other relationship, I'd put up with behavior I didn't like until I reached a breaking point, and then I would fall out of love. When I was done, I was done, even though in most cases I usually stayed much longer than I should have. My pattern had always been that when I couldn't deal with my real feelings, I'd just shut down and retreat from the relationship. I wasn't going to do that now. By this point, we had been together for almost five years, and during that time we had been through so much—Jenny's relapses, her getting her master's degree, me going back to school, and me transitioning from female to male. We'd already had a lot of history together, to say the least.

Now, after months of incredibly painful therapy sessions, and barely getting by at home, we finally had a breakthrough that allowed us to begin mending our broken relationship. We were in therapy and Jenny was talking about how I had changed and wasn't sweet anymore, for what felt like the hundredth time.

With hindsight it's easy for me to see why she thought I had changed so much, because I had, in relation to her and our relationship. I had become angry and mistrusting and I had completely shut down all of my feelings toward her, which, having never seen me like that before, she naturally assumed was because of my transition, which some of it was. As Jenny was saying all of this, it struck me that while I was admittedly emotionally shut down, she had also been very cold and distant toward me as well.

When she finished talking, I said, "I don't feel any love coming from you, either—you've changed toward me, too."

Jenny took a minute to process what I had said and then burst into tears, and said, "I miss you, I miss the person I fell in love with! That small female part of you is gone and I'm angry."

When Jenny finally understood what she was really feeling and I was able to really hear her without being defensive, we were finally ready to begin to heal our relationship.

Over the next several months, throughout the process of writing this book, Jenny and I had to re-learn how to be together. Some of Jenny's habits were now driving me crazy (she can nag, for instance). Before my transition, I let this roll off my back. But now I found myself more impatient and quicker to become angry.

We both made an effort. I slowly began to understand and accept that I had changed. I didn't have to fight or defend against it. But we both had to accept that there were real differences in our dynamic, changes for both of us. For her part, Jenny felt I was yelling at her, when in fact my voice was just deeper and louder. She also felt I was being "aggressive," when in my mind

I was just being direct and forthright. I realized I had to watch how I use my voice and body.

Men and women are very different from one another and thus create a dynamic in a relationship that is quite different from the one two women create. Though I feel very much the same emotionally as I did before my transition, with testosterone on board, I sometimes react to situations differently. This is not a bad thing; it's just one feature that can take some time to get used to. Differences between the sexes, in my opinion, are what attract us to each other in heterosexual relationships and help create intensity and passion. But, for Jenny and me, this shift took some time to adjust to.

These past two years, since starting my transition, have been an intense and exhilarating ride, both for me personally and for us as a couple. I'm extraordinarily proud of the work that Jenny and I did to get our relationship back on track again. Jenny has gone through her own set of changes during this process, and while she struggled at times, she is, and has always been, ultimately happy that I transitioned. In most ways, it has been really positive for our relationship. Many of her other issues with me—that I wasn't motivated, that I was awkward in social situations and shy—don't exist or have lessened significantly. She is also sober for almost a year now. Jenny and I are in a good place. So much has changed: we began our relationship seemingly as two women, and now we are not. In many ways, Jenny and I had to start all over again. We got a do-over.

When I finally began the process of transitioning, some of the things that once scared me did end up happening. For instance, I know that there are people out there who think I am crazy or sick for transitioning. Some people just don't understand. And I've heard people on the radio or on television making fun of me, and yet now I honestly don't care.

In a lot of ways transitioning feels like starting my life all over again. All of my relationships are different in one way or another. Jenny and I have had to transition together. And even though it was painful for me while my mom went through her own grieving process over my decision and was barely able to speak to me and couldn't see me for almost a year, I was able to get through it.

Her process of accepting my transition continues to move forward. We've seen each other several times over the past year. She even said to David Letterman on the *Late Show*, "I really like being a woman and I like my body. If I woke up in a man's body, I would think 'Oh my god, I've got to get out of here,' and that's the way Chaz felt."

I think talking about my transition publicly has further helped my mom come to terms with the fact that I am now a man, but I think there is still room to grow. This is hard for any parent to accept, and for my mom and me it's a work in progress.

In January, *Becoming Chaz* premiered at the Sundance Film Festival. This alone was a huge highlight in my life. At Sundance, the film was then received with overwhelming positivity from the audience and the critics, but getting a standing ovation on opening night was more than I could have imagined. The film, which had its world television debut on the Oprah Winfrey Network's documentary film club, has been one of the many gifts that have come from finally summoning the courage to be myself. What a long, strange trip it's been.

If you're letting fear stop you from transitioning, or from doing something else that you've always wanted or needed to do, then don't. Fears are not facts. With a little time and effort, they can be overcome, worked through, and conquered. As Franklin D. Roosevelt so wisely said, "The only thing we have to fear is fear itself."

Afterword

I had no idea that life could be so easy, or that I could feel so happy and so at peace. If I knew how transitioning was going to change the quality of my life, I would have done it years ago—but I didn't know a lot of things. I didn't know how hard my life had been to live until I had something else to compare it to. I didn't know how disjointed I felt until I became whole. I didn't know how disconnected I was from my physical body until I was finally able to inhabit it.

Throughout the years that I agonized about whether or not to transition, I researched the subject thoroughly. I knew once I started taking testosterone that my voice would deepen, my sex drive would increase, and my face and body would begin to grow hair and muscle mass. I knew that I could change emotionally as well, potentially becoming more aggressive and more confident, and that my reasoning could become more linear and my thought process more logical. I also knew what to expect after having top surgery, how my chest would most likely look, where the scars would be and where my newly constructed nipples would be placed.

What I didn't anticipate, and could never have prepared for, was that I would feel so good, so whole and complete, and that by comparison, through my new set of glasses, I would truly see how difficult and often painful my life had been before transition. Along with going through all of the changes that have happened as a result of transitioning, I have also experienced a deep sense of loss and profound sadness for the forty years of life I spent inside of the wrong body. In addition to the elation that I have felt while becoming the man I was always meant to be, I have had to grieve that my life is half over and I am only now feeling like a complete human being. I grieve for my lost youth, for the boy and young man that I didn't get to be, and I grieve because I will never experience what it's like to grow up as a man, only what it's like to grow old as one.

In spite of this sense of loss, which has now diminished greatly, I am more grateful than words can express for my life, and am happier and more fulfilled than I've ever been. When I do have those momentary pangs of sadness, I turn to my spiritual belief system and summon the faith to put my life back into a positive perspective.

I believe that all human beings are here for a reason, that we are capable of great spiritual growth and can effect miraculous positive change for ourselves and others—I believe in a loving God, a higher power, who delights in diversity and has only our best interests at heart. I also believe that we can use the challenges we've experienced to become wiser and more compassionate, and that it is an honor and an obligation to utilize these life experiences to help others who are challenged by issues we have already overcome.

My life has been an extraordinary journey so far, and while it hasn't been an easy life, it has certainly been a good one.

ACKNOWLEDGEMENTS

I would like to thank a number of people who helped me bring this book to fruition:

Carrie Thornton, my editor at Dutton, who supported, encouraged, and believed in me throughout the editorial process.

Loretta Barrett, my agent, who stood by me for this, my most challenging book yet.

Billie Fitzpatrick, my writing collaborator, who once again masterfully helped me take all of what was inside of me and put it into the pages of this book.

Dina Lapolt, my good friend and lawyer, for all her sage support and advice.

Howard Bragman, my publicist, who is tireless and generous with his expertise.

And Jenny Elia, who, as my partner, has contributed her creativity, passion, laughter, and love during this long haul.

I would also like to thank others who contributed so much to me and to this book, including Christine Ball, Stephanie Hitchcock, and Linda Cowen.

I am especially grateful for all of my family and friends—you know who you are—who have inspired me, encouraged me, and believed in me. Thank you.

RESOURCES

Useful Websites

www.Chazbono.net

National Center for Transgender Equality
http://www.transequality.org
(202) 903-0112

Transgender Law Center
http://www
.transgenderlawcenter.org
(202) 903-0112

FTM International
http://ftmi.org

FTM Alliance of Los Angeles
http://ftmalliance.org

TransYouth Family Allies
http://www.imatyfa.org
(888) 462-8932

National Gay & Lesbian Taskforce—Transgender Civil Project
http://www.thetaskforce.org/
issues/transgender
(202) 393-5177

Gay & Lesbian Alliance Against Defamation— Transgender Terminology

http://www.glaad.org
(323) 933-2240

Parents, Families and Friends of Lesbians and Gays (PFLAG)—Transgender Network
http://community.pflag.org
(202) 467-8180

Gender Spectrum
www.genderspectrum.org
(510) 567-3977

Transforming Family
www.transformingfamily.org

Books

She's Not There (Broadway, 2004) by Jennifer Finney Boylan

The Riddle of Gender (Anchor, 2006) by Deborah Rudacille

Becoming a Visible Man (Vanderbilt Press, 2004) by Jamison Green

Just Add Hormones (Beacon, 2006) by Matt Kailey

Body Alchemy (Cleis, 1996) by
  Loren Cameron
The Transgender Child (Cleis,
  2008) by Stephanie Brill and
  Rachel Pepper
*Gender Outlaw: On Men, Women
  and the Rest of Us* (Routledge,
  1994) by Kate Bornstein
My Gender Workbook (Routledge,
  1998) by Kate Bornstein
*Evolution's Rainbow: Diversity,
  Gender, and Sexuality in
  Nature and People* (University
  of California Press, 2004) by
  Joan Roughgarden
Transgender History (Avalon,
  2008) by Susan Stryker

Films

Beautiful Boxer
Becoming Chaz
A Boy Named Sue
Boys Don't Cry
*A Girl Like Me: The Gwen Araujo
  Story*
My Life in Pink (Ma Vie en Rose)
Normal
Prodigal Sons
Sex-Change Hospital
Soldier's Girl
Southern Comfort
Transamerica
TransGeneration
You Don't Know Dick

ABOUT THE AUTHORS

Chaz Bono is the only child of Sonny Bono and Cher, and for the past fifteen years, an active GLBT rights advocate, author, and speaker. An acclaimed author, Chaz has written two books: *Family Outing: A Guide to the Coming-Out Process for Gays, Lesbians, and Their Families* and *The End of Innocence: A Memoir*. He lives with his girlfriend in Los Angeles.

Billie Fitzpatrick is a writer and book collaborator. She cowrote Chaz's first book, *Family Outing*. Billie lives with her family near Boston, Massachusetts.